Elisha Cooper

CRAWLING

Elisha Cooper is the author of the children's books *A Good Night Walk*, *Beach*, *Ice Cream*, *Magic Thinks Big*, *Dance!*, and of *A Year in New York*. He lives in New York with his wife and two daughters.

www.elishacooper.com

CRAWLING

—a father's first year—

ELISHA COOPER

Anchor Books
A Division of Random House, Inc.
New York

FIRST ANCHOR BOOKS EDITION, SEPTEMBER 2007

The Library of Congress has cataloged the Pantheon edition as follows:
Cooper, Elisha.
Crawling : a father's first year / Elisha Cooper.
p. cm.
I. Title.
PS3553.O5823C73 2006
813'.6—dc22 2006043209

Anchor ISBN: 978-0-307-38718-9

Book design by M. Kristen Bearse

www.anchorbooks.com

Printed in the United States of America
10 9 8 7 6 5 4 3

For Elise

Praise for Elisha Cooper's CRAWLING

"Moving and funny. . . . Anyone who has been a father or mother will appreciate the candor, the whimsy and the ardor Cooper puts into this little keeper."

—*Deseret News* (Salt Lake City)

"Rewarding . . . honest. . . . Elisha Cooper's book of essays on fatherhood is a triumph."

—*The Free Lance-Star* (Fredericksburg, VA)

"Frank and touching and funny."   —*Contra Costa Times*

"Cooper's writing is gentle and warm; like hot chocolate with marshmallows, yet there's a pleasant piquancy to it, as well. This isn't sloppy sentimentalism, but real love that spills onto every page."   —*The Oakland Tribune*

"A memoir [that is] tender to the bone but also blunt."

—*East Bay Express*

"Original, witty and written from the unique viewpoint of a male perspective."   —*Tucson Citizen*

"Amusing and tender."   —*The Hartford Courant*

CONTENTS

CONTENTS

CRAWLING

—birth—

There's a head sticking out of my best friend. This is insane. Anybody who says this moment is the most precious wonderful thing in the world is delusional. This isn't a miracle, it's assault. I'd call 911 but we're already in a hospital.

I didn't know it would be like this, not even the day before. After Elise's water broke in the morning we went for a walk. Elise's belly was poking out from her small body like a melon. We hiked up in the hills and looked out at the San Francisco Bay shimmering in the distance. In the afternoon we drove to the hospital and were given a room with a view of the Oakland hills, and backless gowns. This was nice, I thought.

We walked the halls kicking a ball of tinfoil in an improvised game of soccer. As Elise's contractions increased we stopped playing soccer and just did laps, my arm on her waist. We'd pass the door with the male doctor inside reading *O, The Oprah Magazine*, and Elise would not say much and a minute later when we passed the same door (the doctor a few pages further along in *O*) another contraction would hit, right on time.

Evening became night and night became that time that is neither night nor morning. Elise's contractions got big and painful and the nurse didn't like the baby's heartbeat. She made hushed calls to the attending physician and Elise was hooked to an IV and given oxygen and painkillers. The mood in the room became desperate. Or, I felt desperate. As Elise curled on her side and closed her eyes I felt her slipping from me. My favorite person in the world lay there humming to herself and I could not reach her. I could only hold her hand and be alone with my worry in the dim light of an anonymous hospital room with the taillights of the early morning traffic on the highway outside slowly blinking past.

It got light. Elise got an epidural, I got a coffee. Our ageless Chinese midwife showed up looking rested and cheerful. I like her, but didn't then. After an hour of checking Elise's dilation she said, "Okay, feel like pushing?" Elise, opening her eyes, said, "Yes, *please*."

Elise pushed and turned red. She pushed more and turned burgundy. I held one of her legs and mopped her brow and tried to give her water out of a bottle whose straw kept popping out and onto the floor. And though I had gone to birthing class and done all the correct things to prepare for this exact moment, I couldn't have felt less competent had I been handed three lively cats and told to juggle them. Elise was muttering and I was saying things like "You're doing great" and "You call *that* a push?" Well, no, but it crossed my mind. Everything that shouldn't have been crossing my mind was: how the traffic on the highway outside looked bad today, how soft and pillowy the clouds were, how juggling cats would be difficult, how Elise was now the color of a beet.

Maybe I was trying to distract myself from what was happening. Our ageless Chinese midwife was doing the same, bouncing on the big purple birthing ball across the room between pushes in an attempt to distract Elise, who wanted to push all the time.

Time got tight, focused. Elise was yelling like a wounded animal. I saw the head and thought about calling Emergency. Elise was yelling louder and I was holding her leg and saying God knows what and nurses were circling and hands were reaching in and out and twisting this being that seemed to want to stay right where it was, not ready to join us yet. Then out it came, a gangly thing covered in blood. The thing was turned to me and it looked into my eyes with the hugest, most startled eyes I have ever seen and our eyes locked. I thought, *I know you*.

And in that instant, in the moment when the baby was wrapped and swaddled and brought to Elise's chest, there was a sense that all the pain that had been in that room was already being repaired, the night of tension disappearing in a soothing wash of forgetfulness, memory stitched together so that we could inaccurately look back on this experience with fondness. Indeed, a miracle.

Elise was beaming. I rested my face against hers and we looked into the baby's eyes. Neither of us said anything for a long time. We were too stunned to remember to check the sex. But as the baby was carried across the room, Elise asked, "What is it?" and I can still hear a voice saying, almost as an afterthought, "It's a girl."

The girl is lying three feet to my right now. She's in her bassinet, taking a nap next to my desk. Her hair is dark with light highlights. It waves in places, curling at the back of her neck. She has a round belly, a dimple on her chin like me. She just took a bath and is wrapped in a white blanket. She's making small noises. Her name is Zoë.

—*two becomes three*—

We live in Berkeley in the hills overlooking the bay. The Pacific Ocean is on the horizon. The hills are lined with winding roads and filled with redwood and eucalyptus trees that cast lots of shade. Steep steps with names like Muir Path and Twain Way cut between the roads. Houses are quirky, wooden Arts and Crafts, and have a way of blending into the trees. Over the hills is the Hayward Fault. If California is separate from the rest of the country, and if the Bay Area is separate from the rest of the state, and if Berkeley is separate from the rest of the bay, then the Berkeley hills are separate from the rest of Berkeley. It's the epicenter of isolation. But it's home, for now.

Our apartment is an addition on a large wood-shingled house in the elbow of one of the winding roads. It's one big room with fifteen-foot ceilings, a studio that had been designed for a musician so he could give concerts. Bookcases line two of the walls, though the books aren't ours and neither is the furniture. The only furniture we own is the two desks, planks of plywood on sawhorses, where we work. Elise is getting her Ph.D. in psychology at Cal; I write and illustrate children's books. Across from our desks are floor-to-ceiling windows that open on a garden and a stream. When the windows are open there's no real divide between the inside and the outside and we're often chasing hummingbirds back to safety. It's peaceful except for the opera singer across the stream who practices during the day. Things are so peaceful I'm sure that Zoë's cries, echoing through the concert hall and out the open windows, will wake the entire neighborhood.

When Zoë came out there was a moment, about thirty seconds, when she made no sound. We've heard this is normal but I remember thinking then, "Come on baby, *scream*." Then she did, and her hands fluttered as if she were falling backward in open air. We spent the day calling family and friends, drinking champagne, and learning how to breast-feed. Rather, Elise learned how to breast-feed. I just stared at Zoë whenever she slept on my chest. She kept both fists in front of her face like a boxer and sometimes startled awake and punched me.

After a night in the hospital we walked to the parking lot, shocked we were being allowed to leave, and drove home. In her first week Zoë lowered her fists from her boxing position. She struggled with evenings, though. She bawled and wouldn't take a pacifier. She sucked our arms. There were welts on both our biceps and Elise and I looked like recovering heroin addicts. When even arm-sucking wouldn't calm her, I took Zoë for walks.

I walked into the evening. The summer light was soft, the air sweet with lavender and wisteria. There was the clatter of dishes being cleared, the murmuring of voices, lights clicking on in kitchens as the sun dipped into the bay. A deer stepped across the road before disappearing into shadows with the flick of its tail. Neighbors walked dogs. Something about the outside calmed Zoë. She faced out—I held her in my left arm like a football—and poked me in the ribs with her elbow. I pointed out a neighbor's black-and-white cat, the recycling bins, the oak tree growing through a fence. I pointed out our neighbor's Alexander Calder mobile turning from a living-room ceiling.

But how do you explain the world to someone who has

just come into it? As I talked my words became circular—each explanation requiring another one—and ended up sounding like this: "That mobile is red. What is red? Red is a color, what your face gets when you don't get milk. Milk comes from Elise, and from cows. Cows are bigger than cats, who have claws, as do you, though not really . . ."

It was hopeless. Though as I talked, Zoë fell asleep and her elbow stopped poking into me and I was alone with my worries. I had a few worries about being a parent. A few hundred.

For starters, I had never liked children. Like most men in their twenties, I would sooner have been handed a bomb than a baby. If someone asked me to spend time with their children (no one was asking), I would have felt the same way if they had asked me to spend time with their ferrets. That I wrote books for children was something I chalked up to irony, and chance. After writing a book about New York it was suggested to me by a friend in publishing that I write a children's book. So I did. But I was writing for myself. The books were an excuse to go to baseball games and building sites and draw. There were times that I felt I was writing to the five-year-old me. Him I liked, or at least wanted to reach out to and show a few things and let him know that eighth grade was coming and that he would survive it. And there were times, when I was feeling noble, that I felt I was trying to reach some girl out there, spectacled and curious and lonely, in a library in Topeka. I was writing for her.

So I liked children in my mind, and at some theoretical distance. I just didn't like them in person. I didn't think children were precious and charming and innocent. I didn't like the notion that when something was "for the children" it was beyond discussion. And who would make such an argument? Parents.

I liked parents less than I liked children. I loved my own, and that was it. Parents were baffling to me, another species. None of my friends or Elise's friends were parents. After college we lived in New York, and a young couple, especially in Manhattan, doesn't run into parents except at the door of parties where they were apologizing for leaving early. Parents seemed so frazzled, so entitled, so consumed with being parents. Worse, they seemed unhappy.

In the mornings I got coffee at a café on the Upper West Side that was packed with mothers. The mothers were bent over truck-sized strollers crammed with toys and commandeered by little dictators. These mothers had been editors and lawyers and now they were servants. As they maniacally waved goodbye to their fellow servants and made arrangements for tomorrow's play date and pleaded with little Jonah to *stop doing that*, I'd look at these women and not want children, not want to be a parent. It was a miserable existence, I could tell.

We moved to California for Elise's graduate school, and I kept looking down on parents. I would never be one of *those* people. Elise, because she wanted children and wanted them with me despite my crankiness, waited for me to grow up or at least rant myself out. She must have sensed something I myself couldn't admit. Because as stubborn as I was, in the back of my mind I knew I'd have children someday. I just didn't know how to get there with any grace. I was on one side of a canyon, aware that I'd be on the other side, but had no clue how to make the bridge. And now, I *am* on the other side, and there was no bridge, just this wild biological leap of faith (and some discussion, some unprotected sex). Here I am, a parent. I'm teetering on the edge of the other side, though. I have to learn how to be a parent, to care for this baby. It's terrifying. The only living thing I have ever taken care of was a goat, and that was fifteen years ago, and the goat lived in a stall.

Compounding my anxiety is the awkward and undefined condition of fatherhood. Mothers have issues—a balance of care and work and expectations more complex and difficult than anything men have—but fathers don't *have issues.* We have stereotypes. We're either bare chested and holding a naked baby, throwing a ball on a sunny field with the child as they get older. Or we're potbellied and holding a beer, yelling at the child during a Little League game with beatings and abandonment and years of therapy to follow. So we're either a detergent ad or a deadbeat. Too soft or too hard, with little space in between. As fathers increasingly are involved with raising children, the image of fatherhood hasn't kept up. It's unfortunate we don't have better models—any models—to look toward.

Part of the problem may be that we as men want to hold on to our own images. It's hard to lay a claim to fatherhood when we're so worried about what we think we're giving up. We don't want to lose our idea of ourselves as lone actors. Carefree, caring for nothing. Driving to the mountains, having sex in the afternoon, playing sports whenever we want. How does a baby fit into that? Each new father wonders: will my child let me still be me?

The only thing I knew for certain was that Zoë was stuck in my arms. Here she was, a fact. I reached the bend in the road where I could look out at the bay and Mount Tamalpais looming above it and then I turned around. Night had set in. Bats zigzagged in the now dark blue sky. Ribbons of clouds traced up from the Pacific, airplane lights blip-blip-blipped their way back east, and the moon rose through branches of redwoods over my shoulder. We came home. Zoë nursed, then slept. Elise and I ate. One day over, the next to begin in a few hours. It would be the same, and different. Nursing and napping broken by visits of friends with flowers, neighbors with soup, the UPS man with a package, and yet another fire truck from the Berkeley Fire Department.

Our quiet neighborhood in the hills has had four visits from fire trucks this week. The first came when a neighbor had a seizure and died. The second came when the woman across the road twisted her ankle and had to be carried down her steep front walk (her hill elevator, a common thing in Berkeley, was broken). The third came the following morning, when the elevator repairman caught his leg in the elevator. His ankle snapped—his toes were pointing toward his back. He seemed calm, though, when I brought him a glass of water before the fire truck came and paramedics cut off his jeans and took him away. The fourth fire truck came that night in response to a disturbance up the street, something about a drug overdose. So with all my worries about how Zoë would wake our neighbors, her crying turns out to be quiet in comparison with the wailing sirens from the fire engines.

All the outside drama turns us inward. We stay in our big room and nap and nurse and look out the windows at the trees rustling in the breeze. It feels we are the only people in the world, and two becomes three. We are the image of serenity. If you were to look at us from the outside it would seem that I shouldn't have a worry in the world.

—*a bunny orgy*—

The fucking gifts! The pink cat puzzle, the stuffed green talking turtle, the terra-cotta gnome church, the pajamas with the dog wearing the shit-eating grin, the bushels of secondhand clothes covered in bears, the porcelain box with the porcelain pacifier inside (it breaks, sort of by accident, when it's unwrapped), a pink thing with bunnies whose function I can only guess at, a pink blanket with "*Baby*" written on it in script, a stuffed pig that yells, "*I'm a pig!*" again and again when you squeeze its nose.

Do my friends really have such bad taste? No. Most of these gifts come from family, friends of family, and enemies of good taste. Sure, they were well-meaning (and definitely won't be sending me any gifts soon), though sometimes I wonder. When you give someone a huge plastic toy bus that plays lullabies, isn't that a little passive-aggressive? I'm not even sure who has given us what. We're drowning in stuff. I walk around the minefield of our apartment and without warning step on a stuffed animal that blows up with an explosive *moooo*.

When I lived in New York I worked at *The New Yorker* magazine. One day the art designer and I were working on an issue and she told me how she and her boyfriend had taken a train from the city to meet his parents for the weekend. He had just shaved. But he'd missed a hair, a single black hair on his chin. For the entire trip—as farms and countryside rolled outside and her engaging boyfriend sat talking across from her—she could not keep her eyes off that one hair. Finally she pointed it out. "But, it's just a hair!" he protested, and she replied, "It's all I can see."

So when I look around our place—the sun pouring through open windows on Elise nursing Zoë while music plays—and see a stuffed pink bunny lurking in a corner, it's all I can see (it's just a hare). The problem, though, is that it's *not* the only bunny. There are two other bunnies, and they've had a bunny orgy, and given birth to a tea set, three bibs, and a talking monkey.

It gets worse. Someone gives Zoë an electric swing. I've named it Las Vegas. It has flashing lights and plays showy music and never ever stops. I want to return it but it makes Zoë's eyes open wide, so it stays. When she's not swinging in Vegas I move it behind the couch and cover it with a sheet. Then we're given a stand-up saucer thing. It's the new Vegas. It turns the old Las Vegas into Atlantic City. The saucer thing takes an hour to put together (how can a simple ugly thing be so complex?). Zoë is entranced. She's drawn to what repels me. So it stays, though it's too large to fit under the sheet.

I hate that I hate these things. Here I am, the father of this baby, and I'm letting myself get distracted by tchotchkes! My cares are misplaced. Elise, the psychologist, points out to me that this is all about control. I'm threatened by these gifts because they represent what I cannot control: our home and the new baby that's entered it. I'm in a threatened state of denial over loss of control. Something like that.

I could deal with my issues, but I have a better idea, a plan. A plan to regain control by buying *more* stuffed animals. On the surface this is not rational—how do I hope to stop the deluge by adding to it? But my thinking is this: in a land (house) of scarce resources (floor space) my new, more attractive moose will push out the old, less attractive bunny. Someone must go. It's stuffed animal natural selection. And if I also buy a stuffed cow and a goat and a walrus, this hutch of bunnies has no chance and will soon find itself in the trunk of our car. Clothes will get naturally selected, too. I'll buy nice clothes. After Zoë wears the ugly clothes she's been given, for the day we meet the person who gave it or for the five minutes so we can tell whatever relative she looked lovely in it, they will join the bunnies in the trunk. Then I'll drive to the secondhand stores.

Ever since Zoë was born I have never driven faster (though when she's in the car I drive like a grandmother without her glasses). I'm screeching around corners, rolling through stop signs, a menace. On every errand, there's a clock. As Elise is home taking care of the girl I feel I have an hour to be away. Each minute becomes precious. Traffic jams and Berkeley drivers make me cry and pound the wheel. *Move!* It's not just driving. If there's a line at the post office I don't stand in it. If there's an illegal parking spot I take it. If I go to the art store, where I would normally deliberate over pans of Winsor & Newton watercolor paint and rub my fingers on individual pieces of watercolor paper, I get what I need and am gone. If I work out at the gym it's for fifteen minutes. Then I sprint back to the car. I'm getting lean. I'm always five minutes late.

So when I drive to the secondhand stores, I'm flying. I slow for no speed bumps. I take backstreet shortcuts. And I follow a precise minute-saving routine. First I drive to the secondhand store on College Avenue, which offers the best prices, then to the secondhand store on Solano Avenue, which takes almost anything. Stops are instant. Doors stay unlocked, windows stay down. I throw a quarter in the meter, the bag of stuff over my shoulder, run to the store, sell, run back with a lighter bag and $1.75 in my pocket. After the secondhand stores I race to Goodwill, double-park, run inside to the bin in the back, donate. If the stuff is too strange to donate, or if it's ugly in a funny way, I go to the post office and send it to a friend. I'm hoping they see the humor in this. If the stuff is ugly in an ugly way I leave it on top of the trash can outside of the post office. Some one, somewhere, will love a talking pig.

The finish is at Royal Coffee, where I use the big money I've made on a cup of coffee. The cup is my trophy, what I have won in this crosstown race of selling, donating, and littering. I sit for one minute as the sweat on my T-shirt dries and I feel such a sense of relief, of being cleansed. I am victorious in my battle against the pink things and I will feel this way until the next package or family member with a gift shows up at our door. I know I cannot win (I'm that guy pushing the rock up the hill except my rock is stuffed). But for this moment outside Royal Coffee, I don't mind. Because as much as these trips waste my time, dealing with the gifts has also given me, if unintentionally, time. An hour—windows down and music up—alone. As I run back to my car I see that racing around town has become my downtime.

In the month before Zoë was born, I carved a mobile. I sat in the sun in the garden out back and whittled wood. I carved animals from California—a bear, an elephant seal, a cow, a dolphin, a salmon, a hummingbird. Shavings curled around me. I only stopped to drink lemonade. When I was done carving (it took two weeks), I painted the animals. Then I drilled holes in their backs, tied fishing line to the holes, and the fishing line to small dowels. With the tips of my fingers I pushed the lines back and forth along the length of a dowel, trying as best as I could to calibrate the weight of an elephant seal against that of a hummingbird. I sealed the lines with glue, adding a drop to bring the animals into equilibrium. It was a long process, involving patience I normally don't have. When the mobile was done I hung it upstairs over the new changing table. The balance was near perfect.

This mobile was my gift to the child we were going to have. It was a gift—in anticipation of the pink plastic tsunami that lay ahead—that I wanted to be handmade and beautiful. But it was just as much, I knew even then, a gift to myself. A gift of time. It gave me the space to sit and concentrate on something small, to let my mind wander, and in its wanderings, come to terms with how we were about to have a child and how our lives were about to change.

Elise was doing the same thing, working inside on her dissertation and putting together a changing table. When we were through writing and whittling, we'd check in on each other. We'd walk up in the hills or to the pool in Strawberry Canyon where we would swim or lie on the grass. Or we'd drive to Royal Coffee and sit outside with iced coffees and read, repeating lines we thought the other might like. We talked, but just as much didn't talk, leaving things unsaid as we waited for the day to come. It was a month-long deep breath. And when we looked up from our books we'd watch the people who walked past and try to guess who they were: *that's a banker with mother issues, that's the troublesome member of a bean cooperative, that's a father selling his baby's stuffed toys.*

I miss the slow ease of those days, but how can you miss a time you don't have time to remember?

—the sous-chef parent—

In her first days, Zoë slept in the bed between us. She woke every two hours to nurse and reportedly I would get up on my elbow and say, "What can I do?" before falling back into my pillow without waking up. The night belonged to Elise. She had endurance. I didn't.

When I met Elise in college I fell for her because she was a great athlete (and she looked great in soccer shorts). She was an All-Ivy soccer player and I'd go to her games and watch her run circles around her defenders, curly auburn hair bobbing like crazy, and I was amazed that she would never ever stop. This was someone I should chase, I thought. When I saw her in the training room getting her ankles taped, my ankles started feeling bad and I found myself at the training table next to her before my own practice getting my ankles taped, too. I babbled about whatever and she smiled and raised her eyebrows. She had, and has, piercing blue eyes. That she saw through me with them and didn't let on, and dumped her boyfriend to go out with me, says something I think about her kindness, and ruthlessness.

After college Elise took up running, placing in the top fifty women in the New York City Marathon. When we run together in the hills behind our house she leaves me far behind, panting and scheming how to reel her back to me so I can slip rocks into her shoes. Every year her running team does this outrageous relay race, from Calistoga to Santa Cruz, 199 miles through San Francisco and the night. She was running eight days after giving birth. She's that kind of woman. When presented with a challenge—such as a hungry baby at three in the morning—she just *does*.

So Elise is able to make it through the night. I'm able to make it through the night, too. I'm sleeping. I should be sleeping worse, I really should. I almost wish I were sleeping worse if only out of a sense of solidarity (okay, not really). When morning comes I feel like I'm meeting Elise at the end of the marathon and we're standing around and talking about what a long hard race it was though the fact is that I took the bus.

After a month, Zoë started nursing every three hours, then every two hours, then one. She was nursing because she could. Elise said it was like Zoë was sleeping in the refrigerator. One night, the refrigerator had had enough. There was a lot of crying, which I slept through. In the morning I tried to guess what happened. "Last night was *tough*?" I said. Then I listened to Elise's plan to banish Zoë to her bassinet, stifled a fake yawn, and said, "Sounds good!"

We placed the bassinet at the head of the bed. After watching *SportsCenter* I'd lie on my stomach and look at Zoë as she slept, her features calm in the soft light of the changing-table lamp, both hands up in surrender.

Zoë slept better and then she didn't. She got a rash on her face and would scratch and wake herself. Elise tucked Zoë's arms to her sides with a blanket. Her rash cleared and there was peace, for a week. She grew, and started banging the sides of the bassinet like she wanted to be let out. She even woke me up.

I lay in the dark and listened. From the other side of the bed I heard a finally fed-up voice say, "Your turn." So I took Zoë and stood in the windows and looked at the branches of the trees waving against the sky as night slipped toward dawn. The trees looked so sleepy. I almost nodded off standing there. Then Zoë fell asleep and I laid her back in the bassinet. Morning came and I said to Elise, "Last night *was* tough!" We decided to kick Zoë out to the crib.

The crib is really just the landing on the stairs behind our bed. Before Zoë was born I extended the landing, hammering two-by-fours together to create a frame and laying a futon on top. It's pretty makeshift. We call it the nook. I fastened a gate on the open side so Zoë wouldn't tumble down the stairs. I did the screwing while Elise was nursing, and though I'm not happy being the man who builds while the woman nurtures, that's what I am. The only problem is I'm no good at building.

Being Zoë's father seems defined by what I can*not* do. I can't soothe her. I can't nurse her. I can't put her to sleep well. I do what I can, though. I bring Elise water. I adjust pillows, fold blankets. I put on music and answer the phone. I ask what I hope are insightful questions. I nod at the answers. I clean Zoë's dirty onesies, which she seems to poop through every hour (we use the phrase "poop through," though it would be more accurate to say "explode everywhere" because it seems as if a small and vigorous flamenco dancer has been stomping on mustard packets inside her diaper and unleashing an indiscriminate and deadly spray of yellow condiment). After cleaning the onesie in the sink, I hang it to dry in the backyard on a wooden laundry rack, or, when the rack is full, on the azalea bush. The backyard has taken on the appearance of a shanty. I come back in and get Elise another glass of water, clean some dishes, chop onions. I'm the sous-chef parent.

All this doesn't take much time, so I sit and sketch Zoë. But she moves a lot so I give up and just look at her. Then we give her a bath and put her in pajamas and bring her up to the nook to sleep. I want to sleep, too, but there's another onesie to clean and out I go to the backyard shanty. The azalea is full, so I have to use another bush.

At two in the morning Zoë whistles for service. I go up to the nook and bring her down to the night kitchen, Elise. After a week of this the night kitchen decides it's closing. We let Zoë cry. I tuck her in and return to bed and stare at the clock—2:12, 2:17, 2:21—before going up to calm her again, my hand resting on her head as her breathing slows. An hour later she wakes and I repeat the process. It's the same the next night, and the next. Each night, though, she lasts a bit longer than the night before. "Last night was tough," I groan to Elise in the morning through the softness of my pillow.

Zoë is sleeping through the night, almost. At dawn I hear her legs thumping: *bum, bum, bum.* I bring her to our bed to nurse. Sometimes she sleeps afterward, sometimes she stares. If I open my eyes I can see a huge pair of eyes five inches from mine, so I try to keep my eyes closed. If she doesn't sleep I take her back to the nook. I'm not the sous-chef parent after all. I'm the busboy, waiting to bring something more to the table.

In the morning I mumble, "Last night was . . ." before forgetting what I was going to say. Elise is sleeping better, I think. I'm too tired to notice. The days have taken on a dreamy quality. If everything weren't so dreamy maybe I'd come up with some theory of sleep, how it is the single most important thing for new parents, how with sleep there are no rules and just what works, how sleep is *zzzzzzz*. Right now I'm going on fumes. I'm on my knees, crawling. The only good thing about feeling worse is that I can look my wife in the face, even if my eyes are half shut. Elise, as usual, is far ahead of me. She's pacing herself. She's taking naps. She's gotten her second wind while I'm just starting to run.

Today, Zoë woke at five. I stumbled up to the nook and brought her to Elise. She nursed and lay between us, turning and staring. After an hour of this Elise grabbed a blanket and went up to the nook to sleep by herself. There I was in the big bed with this small girl staring at me, and the other girl, the one I've been sleeping with for years, was gone.

—car chases good, kissing scenes bad—

Before Zoë was born, a friend said to me, "Go to all the movies you can now, since you won't be able to later!" This was irritating. Not only because it sounded bad—I love everything about movies, from counting the number of previews to arguing about the film afterward—but because everyone was telling me the exact same thing: you *can't* go to movies, you *can't* go to parties, you *can't* eat out, you *can't* take trips, you *won't* have sex, you will *never* look at a breast the same way. They were all variations on the same sad idea: "Your life as you know it is over." I just nodded at these people, seethed inside, and thought, "Watch me." And I made plans to do all the things these people said I couldn't do, refusing to entertain the possibility that they were right. I was like a kid on his sled at the top of a slope and everybody at the bottom was yelling, "Look out for the trees!" which is why I have pulled my hat over my eyes.

This is why we have come to the movies. Tonight's film has lots of explosions and car chases. Some people in the audience are screaming, some are crying, though not in the way one might expect at the movies. We're in Oakland at the Parkway Theater, which looks like it was cool in the nineteen-thirties. It has an old marquee where individual letters are hung up each week by some guy on a ladder. Above the marquee the PARKWAY sign flashes vertically in red Art Deco neon. Tickets come ripped from a wheel. The Parkway Theater is the type of place where going to the theater is often better than the movie.

Every Monday night the Parkway opens its doors specifically for parents and their newborns. It's called "Baby Brigade." There's only one rule: the baby can't walk. Parents who come early grab the couches near the screen. Latecomers take the lounge chairs in the back. The theater soon fills with baby seats and baby toys and a low-level babbling. Parents walk around with infants on their hips, greeting friends from birthing classes or mothers' groups. In the lobby on a red carpet a line forms for pizza and beer and wine.

The lights go down, the babbling continues. After a

taped announcement from the Parkway's owners urging us not to leave dirty diapers in the beer pitchers, the movie starts. Movies are only a few months past release (admission is five dollars), and a full range are shown. As nudity and violence unfold and erupt on the screen, fathers stand in the back and bounce their babies or hurry to the bathroom to change diapers and to the lobby to get another beer. Everyone is a bit tipsy—except the babies, unless alcohol converts into breast milk fast—drunk more than anything else on the intoxicating fact that we are here at all, at a *movie*!

Each week a babyless couple shows up not knowing it's "Baby Brigade" night. They swivel their heads—surrounded and confused—like a pair of spring-break vacationers who've wandered by mistake into a gospel tent revival. They were looking to make out and have a romantic evening, and what the hell is *this*? To us, *this* has become normal. We're regulars. Every Monday night finds us at the Parkway. Good movie, bad movie, doesn't matter. In fact, it's better if the movie is bad because then we don't care if we miss dialogue when the baby behind us screams. Ear-splitting interruptions actually let me and Elise create dialogue: "What did she say?" "I think she said, 'I love your trousers.' " The more we go, though, the more the crying becomes background noise, like the rattling air-conditioner at an art-house theater. A state of almost-quiet settles in. Parents feed, babies feed. We see one movie with a dream sequence where a tiny man is climbing over an enormous breast and hugging the enormous nipple with both arms— appropriate, as many in the audience are doing just that.

Zoë doesn't nurse enough at the movies. She likes to watch, especially the car chases. One night I looked around us and she was the only baby in the theater with her eyes open. Unfortunately, this movie was a comedy. Lots of laughter and fart jokes. As Zoë kept looking, her eyes grew wide and scared. Then she freaked out. Elise walked her to the lobby and I ate, and then I walked her to the lobby and Elise ate, and then we left. Comedy was not as soothing as action. And romance, with its long meaningful pauses and slow kissing scenes, was the worst. Romance drove Zoë nuts. I'd be watching two attractive actors making out in a stylish Paris apartment, and find myself wishing that a SWAT team would crash through the windows and start shooting the place up. Because if not, Zoë blows up, and keeps blowing up all the way home.

We always come back to the Parkway, though. Tonight is like every Monday night. We've already watched the now familiar don't-put-your-diaper-in-the-beer-pitchers announcement. Elise and I are eating pizza. Zoë is staring at the car chases. Then I take her to the lobby past the row of fathers bouncing their babies to get another glass of wine and on my way back I look to the side and there's the baby-less couple.

I had noticed them when we came in. The man was thin and handsome, with trendy glasses he kept taking off to wipe clean as if he couldn't believe what was going on around him. The woman was blonde and curvy, though it was hard to tell because she was slumped low in her seat as if she wanted to disappear. They hadn't been touching each other. In fact, they had seemed to be studiously keeping some space between them, as if they might conceive if they got any closer. Now they're making out. They're hardly watching the movie. Her hand is playing in his lap, his hand is slung around her neck and moving lightly over her breast, fingering the top button on her shirt. I look at them and think about the nights when Elise and I went out before we had a child, and in that brief moment, I envy the baby-less couple deeply. I envy their ability to sit in the dark and grope each other, to be not balancing another person, to go home and make love without putting someone else to sleep first, to slip in and out. And then in the same breath, I don't envy them, or at least, I'm not bothered that I envy them. I think about how Elise and I have done what they are doing and now we are doing something else. And how this some-thing else—going to a movie with a baby—is pretty cool in its own right. Something we are able to do precisely because we have a baby. Life with a baby is not simply a matter of can or can't, but an odd place in between. As I move on past the babyless couple—they've come up for air, the guy has moved his hand to the other breast—I think that we and they may be on the same hill but just a bit further down the slope.

I return to our couch and hand the girl to Elise and ask her what I missed. "Not much," she says with a smile. I put my arm around her shoulders. Zoë slips a hand up her shirt. We sink into the couch and eat another slice of pizza, the three of us intent on the flickering light of the screen.

— *the first time i drowned my daughter in milk* —

Why are parents so obsessed with the first time their babies do anything? The first smile, the first step, the first word. It's exciting, yes. I get excited, too. But firstism borders on obsession. And, it's inaccurate. So much of parenting has to do with failing, why not remember the bad things? The first time the baby was dropped in the bath, the first time she choked on a prune. In short, why is everything supposed to be *good*? In that spirit, the first time I drowned my daughter in milk was in late September.

Zoë had never taken a bottle. We had a plan to change this. One day Elise went to her office on campus for the morning and left me and Zoë alone. We thought it would be easier to give Zoë a bottle when Elise's breasts were not in the vicinity. I held Zoë in my arms as I warmed the milk and talked with her softly about the fantastic thing she would soon experience. Then I sat in the rocking chair, leaned her back, and inserted the nipple. As the nipple went into Zoë's mouth a sound came out that might be comparable to what would happen if I tried to feed her a cattle prod. This was unnerving. I moved her to another position, turned on some classical music, tried again. The cattle prod wasn't working. Our morning turned into a downward spiral of screams and spilled milk and snot. I was doing something terribly wrong; I wanted to do it again.

Round two came two days later, once Zoë and I had both recovered. Elise went to campus, leaving us alone again. I heated the milk, prepared the soothing nursing environment, inserted the cattle prod. Zoë started bellowing immediately. Again I changed positions but her crying only intensified. I held her too tightly and she pooped and I ran upstairs and changed her diaper, her legs straight and quivering, and because she was on her back she threw up what little milk had gotten into her and gagged and started shrieking as if I was killing her, which I sort of felt like I was, or at least like I wanted to. So I shoved a pacifier into her mouth, which only made her throw up more. I had completely lost my cool. She was furious, I was furious. She was screaming, I was screaming inside. My jaw felt like it was made of steel. Finally, I went for a walk outside as I figured it would be more difficult for me to strangle my daughter and dispose of her body in view of the neighbors.

Parenting is not a competition I am having with Elise, but I do know that if it is one, it is one that I am losing. She's got the biological edge (who wouldn't prefer Elise's breasts?), so I know Zoë's rejection of me isn't personal. But Elise also has something essential I do not have. She has the ability to deal with frustration, while I am a hair trigger away from disaster. I can't shake the feeling that Zoë is on to this. That this is, in fact, personal. I think Zoë senses my frustration and feeds off it as opposed to the milk in the bottle. And what baby would respond to a father who says, "Drink the damn milk, *please!*"?

Round three, a week later. This time doesn't even involve milk—we can fight just for the sake of fighting. Elise and I are at a friend's house in Oakland for dinner. Zoë starts crying and I walk outside to, in theory, calm her. I lose my composure in an instant. It's not quite clear to me why. Even as I halfheartedly sing, let her suck on my arm, point out the moon, she knows I am upset and everything I do just makes her madder. She starts hyperventilating. She's glaring right into my eyes. I'm glaring right back. It's like we're facing each other from either end of a dusty street in a Western and instead of pistols we have similar genes.

I rarely got in fights growing up. The few ones I was in I lost. In second grade it was Casey Neill. I remember both of us grabbing the other one's nose and not letting go (I guess that one was a draw). In fourth grade I got beaten up by a child actor whose child actor brother played the adorable kid in *Terms of Endearment*. In high school, even though I played football, I wasn't that tough. When teammates fought I was the guy who tried to separate everyone and then got squashed himself. In college, where I played football, too, I once lined up across from a defensive back and when he snarled, "I'm going to fuck your mother after the game," I remember thinking, "wait, how does he know my mother?" So I don't think of myself as a fighter.

But here I am in what feels like the fight of my life. A battle with a baby. I'm fighting a thing the size of a Muppet who makes me angrier than I have *ever* been. As I walk down the street in Oakland I am yelling (under my breath though, so as not to arouse suspicion), "*Stop it! Stop crying!*" And just before the urge to throw Zoë into the bushes becomes more than an urge, I think about my goats.

I had five goats on the farm in Connecticut where I grew up. When they were babies I nursed them from a bottle, I milked them every morning once they were grown, and every day I took them for walks. They were well behaved except when they didn't want to be. Sometimes, before coming back to the barn, they would stop and eat my father's apple trees. They weren't supposed to and they knew it. One goat who doesn't want to be caught is difficult to catch; five goats working together are impossible. And a small apple tree can be eaten quickly. So one by one I tackled the goats and dragged them back to the barn hard by their necks. I remember the sound of their hooves scattering the dirt and I remember how scary it felt to get so angry. How easy it was for me to turn into a brute. It was something I felt awful about then, and even now.

When I remember this I realize that while I may not be a fighter, I have a temper. I have the ability to snap, a terrible thing in a parent. I also realize that Zoë, with her grown-up features and full head of hair, is only three months old. I forget that she is not crying to spite me, that I am entirely responsible for her, that she's not a goat. That she's my *daughter*. And I'm caught short.

So I bring Zoë back in my mind from her imaginary trip to the bushes, and bring her close into my arms, and take a deep breath, and think, who am I really fighting? Am I fighting my daughter, or my short temper? The answer is sad and obvious. It's me on me. I'm fighting myself, and taking a pummeling.

What saved me on that street in Oakland was recognizing that at some deep level I am flawed (that and the prospect of jail time), knowing that the flaws I have are my own, and that this girl and I will be joined together for a long long time, for years, and that if I can just ride it out for the next five minutes, and for the five minutes after that, we will be okay and may even ride happily into the Western sunset.

Since I'm probably in denial about the depths of my anger, I take it and redirect it toward others. Specifically, toward strangers who make comments about me and Zoë. These strangers are usually older women. The advice they give is said with a smile and therefore impossible to counter. While mothers get advice, too, comments are more easily directed at fathers, because, being male, *we obviously don't know what we're doing.*

I have a friend who was on a bus in Manhattan with his baby. An older woman approached and told him he was holding the girl incorrectly and could break her neck. Then she turned to the other riders, smiled broadly, and said,

"New father. Doesn't know anything!" Another father I know was having a friendly conversation with a woman at a supermarket in Chicago, but when his baby started crying the woman cooed, "*Ohh*, she must want her mommy!"

Where did this come from, this idea that some women know better and feel entitled to let you know? That fathers are fair game, in need of correction? To those who see a father struggling with a crying baby, he's fine. Well, he's not fine, but he's working things out. He'll be okay. Give him a hand if he asks, or a smile. Do not reach out with a tissue and wipe the baby's nose. And, please, don't give your advice, your condemnation dressed up as help.

When Zoë was a few days old we brought her to her doctor for her first checkup. As I opened the door to the office, a woman on the street saw me, smiled and raised her eyebrows, and said, "That baby needs a *blanket*!" I smiled back, then retreated inside, flummoxed and defeated. What should I have said? What could I have said? When we left the doctor's half an hour later I had a response, but the woman was no longer there. There's the French expression for this: *l'esprit d'escalier*. "The wit of the staircase." The person who halfway down the stairs after a confrontation comes up with the perfect response. We all feel this at times. Caught short, left only with the bitter wish that we could have responded with something smart that would make us feel less small as we tumble toward the ground.

So even as I try to control my temper and avoid a fight with Zoë, I'm angling for a fight with a stranger: *the first time I yelled in public because of my baby.* I'm waiting for someone, somewhere, to say something about how I'm raising this girl wrong. I have possible responses: "That baby needs a *blanket!*" "Okay, can she borrow your shirt?" And, "*Ohh*, she must want her mommy!" "Well, her mommy is dead." Angry? Yes. Reactionary and a little bit crazy? You bet. And of course, making all of this irrelevant is that when this future moment comes it will take me by surprise and I will be so floored I won't know what to say. Later I'll come up with something.

—blueberry scones—

The Cheese Board is the stomach of Berkeley's Gourmet Ghetto. Started in the sixties by a couple of kibbutzniks, it has been feeding the Berkeley community with cheese and bread ever since, along with a healthy serving of piety. It's a collective. The workers look like my parents: sweet, graying, a bit worn, like they have wild stories about the times they spent with Ralph Nader back in the day.

The Cheese Board smells like morning. It's really one big kitchen, with tables covered in flour and dough and ovens opening with warm bread. The smell of bread is as permanent as everything else here: the poster of three big-nosed men smelling a hunk of Parmesan, the wheel of cheese etched in the sidewalk out front, the old lady sitting on the milk crate who nasally mumbles "Spareanychange" to everyone who enters, the wooden benches on either side of the front door, and me. I've been a fixture at the Cheese Board every morning since moving to California.

Some years ago I read in a book that making a perfect painting was easy. You just had to make yourself perfect. I've always been struck by how wonderfully and aggravatingly accurate this is, because painting is as easy, and as difficult, as that. For me, making myself perfect means starting my day at the Cheese Board. I have a routine and I stick to it. I need my special coffee (an extra-strong latte, which is waiting for me when I come to the front of the line because the workers start making it when they see me walk in the door). I need to sit on the wooden benches. I need to read *The New York Times*. I even need to tune out the Spareanychange Lady. She's as much a part of the morning as the coffee and the paper, which combine to make me perfect, filling me like a well so that when I get home I can pour myself into my painting.

The Cheese Board bakes a different scone every day. Blueberry scones are the best but every day is not blueberry. Some days it's raspberry or olallieberry, some days it's nuts. And while this is sort of pathetic, I don't paint as well if the scone of the day is, say, maple pecan. If the Cheese Board runs out of scones I feel empty, and not just in my stomach. I'm thrown when my morning routine is thrown. I don't like to make any compromise. Zoë will have to come with me.

The first time, I slid Zoë into a shoulder sling and we headed down the hill. Six-thirty in the morning, foggy. The early chill of fall. Mist curled through the tops of the pines and the redwoods. Dew covered the grass and beads of water dotted the flower petals. Shafts of light broke through the mist and down to the Berkeley flats below us, turning stucco buildings white and the skyscrapers of San Francisco across the bay into gold. We took the steep steps that shortcut through backyards. Kitchen lights flicked on. Coffee grinders revved. The steps met up with the road, the street flattened along with the neighborhood, and the Cheese Board was two blocks away. But Zoë started hiccuping, then crying, so I took her out of the sling. She sucked on my arm and eventually calmed down and we retreated back up the hill to Elise. So on our first trip to the Cheese Board we didn't get there.

We tried again the next morning. I held my breath as we passed the spot where we had turned around the day before. Then, after releasing my breath, we entered the Cheese Board. I bought a scone and my special coffee. I stood next to the benches and read the paper as Zoë stayed asleep in the sling. I could squeeze her with my arm and increase the volume of her snoring and it was like I was playing an accordion, a celebratory polka. Then I walked back up the hill and started to paint.

This routine continued until Zoë grew too big for the sling. We graduated to the Baby Björn carrier and our walks down the hills became interactive. She stared ahead, waving her arms. At the top of one of the steps there's a lemon bush. I picked a lemon, held it in front of Zoë's nose, then threw it down the steps. She watched as it jumped into someone's yard. Every morning we threw a lemon and the bush started to run out of lemons. We passed a yellow tetherball which we kicked for good luck. Since our timing each day was the same we ran into the same people: the dour man with the fat dog, the cyclist with the dog in his front basket, the old men talking politics and leaning against the newspaper racks in front of Peet's Coffee. I pointed them out to Zoë as we walked past the fancy shoe store, the juice collective, the other fancy shoe store, and then we arrived.

Our time at the Cheese Board became interactive, too. Zoë batted at my coffee cup and I let her mouth the lid. I read her small articles in the paper, like the one where Spain and Morocco were fighting over a three-acre island inhabited by goats. Zoë listened or didn't, or stared at the colorful STOP THE WAR signs in the Cheese Board window. Then we walked to Chez Panisse and looked at the menu. Zoë would paw at it, mouth open, until her mouth slid into a yawn, and she fell asleep on the way back up the hill. I was able to read the rest of *The Times* then—quietly stopping to put down my coffee, turn the page, pick up the coffee, tilt back Zoë's head. I didn't want to wake her, so it took even more time getting home and I found I was starting my work later and later.

The days grew shorter and the girl grew longer, so I retired the Björn. I put Zoë in the jogger. I wrapped her in a blanket since it was cold, and covered her hands with socks. I took the streets. I missed walking down the steps and throwing the lemon. I missed having Zoë against my chest and being able to see what she saw. And the tetherball got stuck. Somebody kicked it too hard and the rope wedged around the pole. When I reached the Cheese Board I bought a scone though they hadn't had blueberry in forever. It'd been pecans for weeks. I couldn't read the paper, as Zoë grabbed the paragraph I was reading, so I tried to distract her with a bread roll. She mouthed the roll, then distracted me by throwing it to the floor and put the paper in her mouth. I gave up and bounced her over my shoulder while she looked at the people coming in and out. On our way up the hill she napped like before, and I spread *The Times* on top of the jogger and read. When it rained I put a plastic cover over the jogger and when we came home I left

Zoë sleeping outside. She looked so peaceful, raindrops clattering above her.

Normally I can't paint if anything around me is unsettled. The right music has to be on, the phone off, nobody can be in the room. Only in the last few years have I made an exception for Elise. But now, with Zoë in the rain and likely to wake in minutes, I just started to work. I picked up my pencil and began to draw, checking outside occasionally to make sure Zoë was asleep.

Acceptance of change is at the heart of parenting, which is not good for someone so bad at it. Change for me has always been a scary and unknown creature, whose circling presence made me construct routines to guard against it. Changing my routine, I was sure, would ruin my art. And yet, that didn't happen. Zoë, by doing nothing more than being on my chest, showed me I could paint when I wasn't perfect. She entered my mornings and broke them down. Last week the espresso machine at the Cheese Board was broken and I came home and made coffee, and since we were out of milk I used some of Elise's breast milk. And that was a change. Now I spend as much time retrieving scones as eating them, kicking tetherballs as reading Maureen Dowd, and I am able to paint just fine.

But it's better than that. All the dawdling, all the lemon picking, all the walking to the Cheese Board and back has, counterintuitively, given me *more*. More space to let my mind wander, more time to picture what I am going to paint, to the point that when I return home my well is spilling over. Imperfect can be better than perfect. If Zoë weren't with me I would have driven.

This morning it was pouring. I tucked Zoë inside my raincoat and we took the route down the steps. The steps were waterfalls and water leaped past us before diving down leaf-clogged drains. Beads of water floated down from the branches above us. The lemon tree had grown more lemons, so I threw one. The tetherball was back down, too. I pointed out the bay through the trees, the dark gray rain clouds above it, the Spareanychange Lady under her umbrella.

As we entered the Cheese Board it was warm with the smell of baking bread, even warmer on a wild day like today. The blueberry scones were back. My special coffee was waiting for me when I got to the front of the line. I sat on the wooden benches outside and ate, bouncing Zoë in my arm as we watched the people of Berkeley come and go. The morning felt the same, and different, as if it had always been this way, and now only more so. Elise met us after her run and I gave Zoë to her and went back inside for another scone, and as I was standing in line I realized I was bouncing the blueberry scone in the crook of my arm.

—*the chicken ranch*—

For our first significant outing with Zoë we went to a base-ball game. I'd been careful to buy seats at Pacific Bell Park under the grandstand, out of the sun and away from foul balls. As Elise and I settled into our great seats, I was pretty pleased that we were taking our baby to a ball game. Then Barry Bonds came to the plate. The crowd got to its feet and Bonds crushed the first pitch and the crowd went wild. The next batter followed with a line drive, and the next. Every-one around us was jumping up and down, slapping high fives. Not everyone. Zoë, under a blanket on Elise's lap, was screaming as if she'd been hit with a bat. The noise was too much. Our seats under the grandstand actually amplified the noise. The Giants never stopped hitting, and after an inning and a half we went home.

A week later we tried another outing. While Elise got a haircut in downtown San Francisco I walked with Zoë to the Museum of Modern Art. I took her to the exhibit of some German Expressionist since I thought she might like the bold flat colors. Ten feet into the exhibit Zoë let out an auditory impersonation of Edvard Munch's *The Scream*. Once I left the gallery, she stopped. In the next exhibit she was quiet until I was deep inside and then, *The Scream*! And again, once we left the exhibit, Zoë stopped. Was it the space? The whispering museumgoers? Did she not like German Expressionists?

My perfect trip would be to Spain, to that festival in Buñol where people throw tomatoes at each other. Zoë's perfect trip might be to a tomato patch where she could watch a dog dig in the dirt. I've had the growing understanding this fall that Zoë keeps us from traveling. Going with her down the hill for a scone is one thing, going with her over the hill and through the woods and up the mountain is another.

Zoë is a baby. The fact that I can't fly away with her to places I went before she was born should be obvious. But the fact that I make these concessions upsets me. I worry she's a liability on my ability to pick up and go. And I fear if

I compromise and don't travel I'll become a person who sits around on his sofa, shackled to home, going nowhere.

In the face of these worries I am doubly insistent we go places. We have to take her to an Oakland Raiders game, we have to take her camping in Yosemite, we have to take her to Bhutan, today! We may not even make these trips, but I want the option. I want to hold on to my idea of limitless horizons, another city another day, with nothing but my passport in my pocket. That life has become more complex makes me resent my daughter. I resent that she can't stay at a baseball game, can't go to a museum, can't pack her own bag. I'm not being fair, of course. And I can always fly away on my own. But there is part of me that wants her to come, to fly to Spain with me and see La Tomatina, and how many months do I have to wait for that?

Elise and I drive to Tomales Bay for the weekend. It's a bright fall day as we head over the Richmond–San Rafael Bridge. In silence we stop and go through the commuter towns of Marin, through shady groves of redwoods and among ochre hills circled by buzzards, then over a cow-filled ridge and down into the Olema Valley. The piney back of Point Reyes rises to the west. As we head north along Tomales Bay, past estuaries and marsh grass ruffled by wind and snowy egrets staring hard into the water, Elise and I release a collective breath. Zoë, who hates riding in the car, slept the whole way.

Some friends gave us their house on Tomales Bay for the weekend. It's called the Chicken Ranch. It's small and wood and white, and looks even smaller in the shade of the gigantic eucalyptus tree that hangs over it. Its porch is twenty feet from the water. After unpacking, Elise and I walk out the rickety gate and head north on the rock shore. We walk next to cypress trees and under old piers. Out on the water we see mergansers and ruddy ducks, pelicans flying an inch off the surface, and an oyster farm across the bay. The sun breaks through the clouds. I adjust Zoë's floppy white hat and am content for the moment.

Friends drive up and join us in the afternoon. We make dinner and Zoë sleeps and we stay up late talking and trying not to laugh too loud, since the Chicken Ranch walls are so thin. In the morning, with Zoë in one hand and a coffee in the other, I stand on the porch and point out a seal popping its head up in the water, the kayakers slipping by in the fog, one of our friends running past, and jumping into the bay naked and scattering the kayakers. It's going to be a good day.

But I want to drive out to South Beach. South Beach is on the ocean side of Point Reyes. Point Reyes is a foggy triangle of land leaning against the coast, and Tomales Bay is the interior of that triangle. Point Reyes is rugged. Grizzlies used to live here and in the eighteen-hundreds Teddy Roosevelt came to hunt them. Once, in a nearby field, a man lassoed a grizzly bear and after some pulling back and forth both man and bear escaped. Eventually the grizzlies were driven away and replaced by cows. Point Reyes was the largest producer of butter in the state and then it wasn't. When the Point Reyes National Seashore was incorporated in the sixties, the dairies were protected. They're still working, the only structures here, and the whole place feels like it never left 1948.

Whales migrate along the coast of Point Reyes. Elephant seals haul up on its beaches. The beaches are wild, and the wildest beach is South Beach. The waves there are monsters. They leave a pit in my stomach, and because they are scary I must swim in them when I'm here. Swimming involves ten minutes of daring whomever I'm with to go in with me, an incredulous tearing off of clothes, a crazed sprint across the beach into ankle-deep water where we kneel, splash freezing water over our heads, and run back. It's not really swimming.

Elise and I were married in Point Reyes. We were married along its southern edge, on a hike with family and friends, in a thistle field at the top of a cliff. Elise changed into a white-flowered dress and had to be carried across the thistles because she had no shoes. I wore sneakers. After the ceremony we went to South Beach and threw footballs and ran around. Some of us "swam." Every time we come to Point Reyes now we go to South Beach.

But today breaks cold and blustery. If it's stormy on the bay it will only be more intense out on the ocean. Zoë won't like the wind. She won't like the drive. Elise and I talk about this, and though I'm willing to cause pain just so we can go to the place we said we were going to go to, I surrender reluctantly to reason and we decide not to drive to South Beach.

We stay at the Chicken Ranch. I sit on the porch. Zoë sits on my lap and we look out at the bay. We look at the small ripply waves and I tell her about the big ones. "Someday you will see waves that are huge, bigger than these," I whisper into the top of her head. I tell her about South Beach. I tell her about Mavericks, the big-wave surf spot down the coast. I tell her about places in the world I've seen, some of the adventures I've had where I was scared but ended out okay. I know she doesn't know what I'm saying, though I hold on to the wishful thought that she can tell it's the voice of someone trying to share the limits of the world. I tell her that someday I will take her to Spain and we will throw tomatoes.

Our friends wake. Our naked friend jumps into the bay again, scattering more wildlife. The morning evolves and all of us stay on the porch, wrapped in blankets and watching the weather. The wind rattles through the eucalyptus tree above us, dropping nuts. It blows the bay into choppy whitecaps, bobbing the ducks and blowing the grass of the fields on the hills across from us where years ago the man lassoed that grizzly bear before letting go. It ruffles Zoë's hair but she doesn't seem to notice. She kneads her fingers around mine and furrows her brow. She's so serious. I think I'm falling in love with her, here on this porch. And my love for her is a small wave, one that will expand and flow, a love that I hope will grow to understand that we don't have to be anywhere but where we are.

—the cutest baby in the world—

Let's face it: most babies aren't that attractive. Zoë is. There's something about her—the big hair, the big eyes— that is striking and almost clichéd. She doesn't look like a baby. If anything she looks sophisticated, which is odd as Elise and I are both sort of funny looking.

Last month on our street a woman walked past us and circled around for a better look and while she was staring at Zoë tripped and fell into a bush. Cars swerve to the side of the road and drivers roll down windows and call out. Women at the Cheese Board surround Zoë and gush, "*Oh, wowwww!*" and light up all the way back to 1967. Passersby leave an eddy of gasps in our wake: "Did you see that *child*?" "That child was a *doll*!" And these are the ones who don't stop to talk, to touch her. It takes time getting anywhere.

We go for walks in the afternoon. Once Zoë gets up from her nap I strap her into the Björn. I look in the tinted windows of parked cars to make sure her hat is on straight (once it took me a moment to notice a couple was inside making out, inches away from our peering faces). As I kiss Zoë's head, she windmills her arms, willing us down the hill toward campus.

The Berkeley campus looks like a forest in which a child threw her blocks. Concrete buildings from the sixties are strewn among redwood groves. A few terra-cotta roofs give color to all the gray and green. The Campanile clock tower stands in the center of campus and the forks of Strawberry Creek run down either side, passing under small bridges and gathering in pools which sometimes bubble with laundry detergent. Paths meander everywhere, opening onto plazas filled with petition-stapled kiosks. Filling out the landscape are the Berkeley students: on cell phones, in groups, suntanning alone on the grass. When classes let out the students stream along the paths in a rush of color.

Zoë steers us along these paths with her fists around my pointer fingers. I'm a motorcycle and my fingers are the handlebars. When I hold a coffee Zoë drives with one hand.

She drives with no hands if I'm reading a magazine, which is dangerous, as once I walk us into a metal pole, the pole passing between her legs and straight into my crotch. Sometimes we stop in clearings and sit on the grass and read, sometimes we go to the library and check out a book. At the gym we watch students play basketball and Zoë is transfixed by the sound of squeaking sneakers. At the practice fields we stand on the sidelines and watch the Cal football team. Players dive after balls and I explain to Zoë what they are doing. Then we walk past the bear statue to the trailhead to meet Elise after her run.

But this is just geography. What really is happening on these walks is we are starring in a movie called *The Cutest Baby in the World*. Female students see Zoë and cry, "*Oh. My. God!*" Male students notice her, too. One football player sees her and says, "*Damn*. She pretty." She is pretty. The thing is, though, *we* are pretty. Attractive women check us out and mouth, "*So cute!*" Faces that would never open up to me, do. The women look into my eyes with a flirtatious directness, a flicker of recognition that what brought this baby into the world was sex.

When Elise was pregnant she got looks all the time. The belly, the breasts. But a woman's fertility is outwardly acceptable, something to be celebrated. The male equivalent isn't, a hidden glance. To be a father and to be viewed as sexual is socially unacceptable, a bit dirty. What these looks do share—for both the pregnant woman and the new father—is that they are sexual without the possibility of sex. They're innocent, a wink.

A few years ago I did some book signings in New York. I sat at a table in a trendy paper store in SoHo as fashionable women strode past, shopping bags on one arm, bald and rich boyfriends or husbands on the other. The women from the Upper East Side wore Burberry jackets and careful makeup. The ones from the Village wore funky hats and carried interesting dogs. Sometimes they smiled and kept walking. Sometimes they stopped and talked and had me draw a caricature of them in a book. The conversations were playful, swaying with innuendo. The women commented on my looks like I wasn't there, leaned into me (boyfriend to the side with the bags and waiting to leave), and whispered secrets that were strange and hilarious and once had to do with spanking. I flirted shamelessly back, anything to sell a book, and had fun calling Elise back home and telling her stories before going back to my "work."

I think, for these women in SoHo, I was a sideways glimpse into some imagined life. The life with an artist, a brooding auteur with a soulful sensibility who lived in a Williamsburg garret. A caricature who made them think about what their life would be like if they had hooked up with some man in their past. I was the road not taken. I was playing a part (I wasn't brooding at all). I could be anyone. Once I realized this, and it didn't take long, I had a friend who was a model and an actor sit in my chair, and for the hour that he sat there he was much better at selling my books than I had been.

For these female Cal students I think I'm a glimpse into their imagined future. I'm the representation of what they want, not now, but sometime later. *The good guy.* The man who loves his wife and carries the baby. This feeling, of desire and hope, hovers for a moment after they pass and then it is gone. I know how transparent these moments are, and how, as with the women in SoHo, these moments are about my imagined qualities. But it doesn't stop me from drinking it up.

Last week, looking to get my daily fill of compliments, I walked with Zoë down the hill to Peet's Coffee. On the way a woman passed us and didn't comment on our beauty and it bothered me. But at Peet's all was normal. I stood in line and acknowledged our many admirers with a little wave, like a beaming politician who is halfheartedly trying to quiet the crowd so he can start his acceptance speech. Then I got my coffee and added sugar and at the exact moment a pretty woman across the room was mouthing the words to me, "*So cute!*" and I was whispering back, "*Thank you!*" I took a gulp. The coffee instantly burned my mouth. Choking, I spat it out on Zoë's head.

That evening I told Elise what happened and she laughed and we talked about how Zoë's beauty had brought out the ugliness in me. Of course, it's nothing Zoë had done. It was just me being shallow. As Elise and I talked we tried to tease apart the beauty we saw in our daughter and the beauty others saw in her, the beauty people attach to babies and the beauty that is sometimes more difficult to bring into focus.

We gave Zoë a bath and I was able to see her whole body, the birthmark at the back of her neck, the gunk between her toes. I could also see her frown better. Her frown may be my favorite thing about her—a furrow that gathers at her brow and reaches through her eyes and into my heart. It's so ornery. As she smacked the water I wondered if this scowl was a glimpse into Zoë's own future. That she will be strong and unsure, difficult and kind. That she will be much more than anyone can possibly know, including us. This would seem obvious, though with a pretty face it's sometimes hard to see.

I can't say I will ever be immune to Zoë's beauty. I still like it when we get looks from cute students on our walks around campus. But as the fall continues I've been trying to keep my pride in check, or at least feel proud of my daughter for who she is and who she will become. When I check in with Elise at night now, we usually end up talking about something Zoë did, how she stuck her thumb up her nose at the precise moment a stranger was saying Zoë was the cutest baby in the world.

—*emergency room, 3 a.m.*—

I woke up Saturday and felt nauseated. Then I threw up. I felt awful but needed to walk Zoë to campus to hand her off to Elise, so I put her in the Björn and headed down the hill and while I was walking past an architecturally eminent wood Arts and Crafts house at the top of Bancroft, I crapped down my leg. There was nothing I could do. It was hilarious, sort of. Me, desperate. The girl, oblivious. And she's the one wearing the diapers.

I spent the afternoon on the couch, feverish and miserable. I didn't even watch football on TV. When Elise and Zoë came home I just lay there. I felt bad that I couldn't help out and worse knowing I'd be getting them sick and the only question was when. For Elise it was Sunday night.

For Zoë it was Monday. She threw up a bit in the afternoon, and then, in the evening, after our doctor had gone home for the day, she threw up a lot. A surreal and cartoonish avalanche of water-cheese that had Elise and me propping her up to keep her from gagging, and saying, "What the fuck was *that?*" The weirdest part was that afterward Zoë smiled. Then she slept. But at midnight she threw up again—Elise and I looked at each other and said, "How is there anything left in her belly?"—and again, soaking her pajamas. It was scary. I called an advice hotline and ten minutes later we packed the girl into the car and were racing to the Children's Hospital emergency room in Oakland.

Emergency room waiting rooms are dismal: the harsh lighting, the claustrophobia. Emergency room waiting rooms for children are doubly dismal: the used toys, the worn attempts at child friendliness, the small sterile chairs (which were sterile at Oakland Children's until Zoë threw up on them). We didn't wait long, though. The receiving nurse was efficient—she'd been seeing sick children her whole life—which oddly made it worse.

We walked past rooms filled with coughing kids and cheery pediatricians. The hospital seemed a strange mix of ill children and hip doctors. Our doctor, wearing an ear stud and glasses with thick black frames, gave us a friendly hello and poked and prodded Zoë. Two nurses stuck her with an excessively long needle (a couple of times, since the first nurse, who was in training, kept missing the vein). Zoë screamed. Elise held her. An IV was connected to Zoë's arm. While all of this was happening there was such a pleading look of desperation in Zoë's eyes. "Why are you not stopping my pain?" she seemed to be saying. While I knew everything being done was the right thing to do, this look pierced me. And everything is worse at two in the morning.

More shots, then some more. Elise curled around Zoë on a gurney and they slept. I sat in a chair and listened to the chatter of the doctors (*Okeydokey, I got room four!*) and the coming and going of Oakland's asthmatic youth (*Oooooaaccchh*). Then it got very quiet—it felt as if I were the only person awake in the entire city—and I watched my daughter and worried.

I don't worry about myself, though sometimes I worry about my bad knees. I joke that I will die getting hit by a bus, a crosstown bus on 42nd Street in Manhattan, because how cool would that sound in an obituary? I don't joke about Zoë getting hit by a bus. I worry it will happen. In flashes, at odd moments, I worry she will die. All parents feel this, a worry that is deep and intractable, understandable and irrational both. It's why we check the crib. Is she breathing? Yes. I think.

In the face of my fears I tell them to Elise. But my worries seep back, an undercurrent of unease. I worry about being a parent whose child dies young: crash, cancer, crossfire. I don't want to be one of those parents. Nobody does. I also worry that my worry is self-centered, since I'm probably thinking about my own grief. And I worry my worry is guilt, because I'm sure if anything happened to my child I will have caused it: lent her the car, moved our family next to a nuclear-power plant, traveled to a country in the midst of an insurgency. My feelings are not entirely selfish. I'm beginning to understand the parental sentiment—which I always thought unhinged and untrue—that I would give my life for my child.

I look at Zoë on the gurney and make a little deal. If she gets better, if she won't look at me with that pleading look again, I will do, *what*? Anything. I don't know what I would give and don't know who I would give it to, but I am willing to find out. Just show me. As I say these words to myself I'm shocked to realize I'm praying.

I'm not religious at all. I had a classic seventies religious upbringing. When I sang in a church choir it was for the singing. When we planted flowers on Easter it was for the horticulture. When I found out I had Jewish ancestors it was interesting culturally. But now I am reaching out to

God, Yahweh, Allah, Buddha, and the Spareanychange Lady, who for all I know is God in disguise. I want to make a pact. I will be a better person, sacrifice anything, my life for hers even, if that will bring her back to health. Please, *make my child well.*

It's not rational. Modern medicine and antibiotics will make Zoë well. And she's not that sick. This is nothing, a stomach bug. I even know that once Zoë gets better I will forget this moment. But right now, here in the 3 a.m. quiet of this nondescript room in the children's hospital in Oakland, I am waiting for an answer that will bring peace to my worry. Worry is the wrapping that comes with the baby. And, as the child grows, the cause of all the prayers we make to ensure she keeps living.

Our ear-stud doctor, as cheerful at dawn as he was at midnight, enters the room and checks on Zoë and checks us out. We wrap her in blankets and drive through deserted streets back home.

Within days, Zoë grows back her belly. In fact, she's getting fat. She's smiling and making an odd cawing sound. I call the sound the dying crow. After a day the "crow" develops a hiccup and it's more like a crow choking on something. She's been crying differently, too, low and gut-tural, like a cement mixer. Sometimes she punctuates her cries with a shriek and it's a cement mixer running over a cat. This shriek is short-lived, though, and the crow comes back to life, which is fine, as carrying a dying cat made it difficult to be out in public. Then the crow dies again, or at least changes to a hacking growl, an old cat with a smoking problem. When I listen to Zoë now, trying to describe the sound she makes and wondering what will come next, it's difficult to even remember my worry and prayers from a few nights ago, which may be the point.

—sportscenter & the beastie boys—

What will we dress Zoë in this morning? Red pants or green pants, white sweater or blue jacket, socks with stripes or socks with dots? As Zoë has become less of a baby and more of a girl, and as it's cold now and she needs more layers, dressing her has become a whole process, and an opportunity for conflict. Elise has favorite clothes for Zoë. So do I. Which of us gets to dress her depends on who we are seeing that day. Elise puts her in the dress covered in farm animals if she's meeting her faculty members. I put her in the blue-and-white-striped thing if we're meeting, well, I don't have anyone to meet. Other days, Elise and I battle. A few times I find myself, once Elise has left for the morning, changing Zoë out of what she's wearing into something else.

Before Zoë was born I spent an evening with a friend and his baby girl while Elise went for a walk with the girl's mother. The friend and I began the evening sharing a Miller High Life forty, and the rest of the evening propping the forty against the baby and encouraging her to mouth the rim, then filming it. When Elise and the baby's mother came back we showed them the clip. They were not as amused as we were. Around this time Elise and I had been discussing the possibility of becoming parents, and this experience with the High Life, perverse as it was, was pretty significant for me. It was a relief to realize that to be a parent you didn't have to be perfect. In fact, you could be pretty bad.

Elise is a good influence on Zoë. She's the one who consults the books, who knows how to treat a rash and when to start Zoë on solid food. As a psychologist she's aware of the nuances of child development. It's not just competence. Elise does the sweet things well, too, like singing lullabies to Zoë at bedtime or sewing a tail on her brown pajamas to turn her into a dormouse for Halloween. I'm sure Elise has faults as a parent, though I'm not sure what they are. Unfortunately for Zoë, she has another parent. And when Elise walks to campus in the morning it is that parent who takes care of her, at least for a couple hours.

"Have a nice morning!" Elise calls from the door. We will. I wait until she's out of earshot and then crank up the rap. I put on the Beastie Boys' "Body Movin'" and dance around the apartment with Zoë in my arms. When I change her diaper I put on OutKast's "So Fresh, So Clean." I make up bad raps in front of the mirror. Zoë cackles and thumps her feet. She probably just likes it that I like it but I don't care. When I get tired I sit with her on the floor and put on Pete Seeger and Woody Guthrie. I play Guthrie's "Car Song," which is repetitive in that annoying way that fires directly onto the brain so I call friends and leave the song on their answering machines.

For lunch I have a peanut-butter-and-jelly tortilla and a Coke, the same lunch I've been eating for years. Zoë sucks the Coke can. She likes this so much I duct-tape shut the top of one can—putting some pine nuts inside for sound—and she has her own Coke-can rattle. As she shakes it I hold her in my lap and we watch English Premier League soccer on television. There's always a game on. I point out the ball as it bounces across the screen and when someone scores, which, this being soccer, never happens, I yell "Goooooll-laaa!" at the top of my lungs. Zoë is captivated. This is educational, I think. I get to watch diving Brazilians arguing with petulant Frenchmen in a stadium packed with beer-sogged hooligans, Zoë gets to watch figures in colorful jerseys running after a ball. After the game we watch football highlights on *SportsCenter*.

When I hear Elise's footsteps outside I turn off the TV and whisper to Zoë, "*Shh*, don't tell." Elise finds us sitting quietly on the couch with an unopened book and asks what we've been doing and I say, "Oh, not much." Elise knows I'm not telling the truth but Zoë won't tell because she can't talk.

If only my bad influence was confined to bad food and bad television. To me, "fuck" is a noun, a verb, a gerund. I think Zoë's first word will either be "fuck" or "fucker." When I walk down the street I look at people and make comments under my breath: "Nice trucker hat, fucker." The problem is, I'm muttering this into the top of Zoë's head. I'm convinced I'm going to be the parent of the kid in kindergarten who corrupts all the other kids. My favorite joke has a punch line about moose cock. It is the funniest joke in the world, trust me. It's the type of joke that improves with time. People who know this joke start laughing at the beginning of the joke. I've told it so many times with Zoë in my arms that maybe Zoë's first words won't be "fuck" or "fucker" after all but "moose cock."

At dinner I talk with Elise about what we did that day, people we met, something we saw. Often my stories have to do with the odd people who live in Berkeley, especially those who shop at Berkeley Bowl Marketplace. My peeve of the moment is when people wear their bike helmets indoors. I mention this to Elise and get all worked up: "These idiots think they're going to crash into the fucking tomatoes!" Hearing myself sound this cranky, I wonder what will happen when Zoë begins to understand my words and not just my tone. Will I stop then? Years from now as we're sitting around our kitchen table, will I tell my family about that motherfucker in the S.U.V. who almost hit me, or will I wait until Zoë has cleared her plate?

It would really suck to censor myself around my daughter. That said, I can probably cut out "fuck." I can watch less television with her. I can cut down on, or at least use more judiciously, my scorn. Because if I don't edit myself a little bit, I fear my daughter will turn into a bad-food-eating, Coke-drinking, rap-playing, sports-watching, profanity-spewing misanthrope. The terrible thing, though, which I can barely admit to myself, is that my greater fear is that she won't.

This morning there is music playing that Elise put on, the Bach cello suites with Yo-Yo Ma. As she gets dressed and ready to walk to campus for the morning she asks what we will do and I say, "Oh, I don't know." But I do know.

There's an English Premier League soccer game that comes on at eleven, a great matchup between Arsenal and Manchester United. Our peanut-butter-and-jelly tortilla lunch comes at halftime, and then we'll dance to the Beastie Boys. Zoë will rattle her Coke can (though I am making pesto tonight and may need to take back the pine nuts). There is something that needs to be done first, though. Elise dressed Zoë in a puffy cream-colored sweater. The sleeves are long, so just the tips of her fingers stick out and she looks like a model, or a sheep. The sweater, actually, is all right. But the striped socks she's wearing are all wrong. That's okay, because as soon as Elise is out the door, I will change them.

—a place at the table—

Entering the café at Chez Panisse is like being welcomed into the kitchen of an old friend. After passing under a big pine tree and through a broad wooden door you walk upstairs into the café. The light is warm and low, reflecting off walls hung with prints of avocados and radishes, and posters of César, Fanny, and Panisse, the characters in the Pagnol films that gave the restaurant its name. The waiters are attractive, gliding under wooden rafters and placing plates on white tablecloths. Diners, dressed up or not, talk over menus. Chefs clatter around the open kitchen, chopping herbs or sliding dishes onto the brick counter. With all this activity, the café is neither too loud nor too soft, but bubbling, like a soup.

If Chez Panisse is an old friend's kitchen it's one where you wouldn't mind staying to help clean the dishes. It's homey, if home were a place that served excellent expensive food. The café has the odd combination of feeling both special and familiar, accommodating an occasion or none at all. It's where Elise and I go on birthdays, but also where we've gone late on a random Tuesday for dessert. It's where we went last year a few minutes after finding out Elise was pregnant. And it's where we came, three weeks after Zoë was born, to celebrate our new addition.

The maître d' with the trim beard knew us (or looked like he wanted us to think that he knew us) and ushered us to our table. I knew him from seeing him reading the paper at the Cheese Board every morning. As we sat I saw the flitting figure of Alice Waters, the owner. She's short, and her trademark flat-topped hat gave her the effect, as she dashed about greeting customers, of looking like a mobile side table. I wanted to rest my glass on her head.

We read the menu, grilling our waiter with questions: "What's a *cardoon*?" We ate a nettle frittata, risotto, lamb. We drank a bottle of wine. Zoë, who was with us, drank breast milk.

We hardly noticed her. She was like an infinitely charming, occasionally active handbag we just happened to be carrying with us on our night out. As she nursed and slept, we spilled olive oil on her. When she woke she blinked, and mouthed a spoon. Our waiter had had a baby recently and when she saw ours we shared stories and at her suggestion changed Zoë on a bench next to the table. For dessert we had apple tart. It was a wonderful evening out, made better because our daughter was with us. This was how I hoped it would be.

A year ago we flew to Paris to visit a couple of old friends. He's a tall balding journalist with a permanent grin, she's a charming and argumentative social activist. They had just had their first child. At night we went out to dinner—brasseries in the Marais where our friends were regulars and where the waiters, after inquiring as to the health of everyone's families, guided us to seats away from smokers or to a couch where we could lay the sleeping baby. The owners would join us and pull up chairs, admiring the baby while telling us what was good to eat that day. We ate and argued, as usual, and I suppressed the urge to throw food at my argumentative friend, as usual. We had a great time.

Having the baby along felt natural and seamless; we were the same friends with an appendage. This trip to Paris, along with the time I helped my other friend film his baby girl drinking a forty of beer, made me want to have a child. It could be done gracefully, I thought.

There's an American disconnection between being an adult and being an adult with children, and no more so than when eating out. Parents teeter between two worlds. They go out to nice restaurants as a couple, or they go to family-friendly restaurants with their children. Family restaurants make my stomach turn: the high chairs, the crayons, the parking lot clogged with minivans, the special menus, the *plastic* (are all my fears of being a parent just a fear of plastic?). Even the expression "family-friendly" makes me queasy because what it also means is "people-without-children-*unfriendly*."

As usual, I blame the parents. I blame parents for being unable to control their children. It's not entirely their fault, though. I also blame restaurants who won't tolerate the slightest bad behavior. And I blame all of us who have ever given that "You brought that child in *here*?" look to a parent who was having a rough time. Family restaurants are the response to that look. The refuge for parents who can't control mayhem and the refuge for parents who don't want to be scorned. Which came first, the hurled chicken wing or the embarrassed broken egg? The result is the same. Families are isolated from the rest of society. As child-driven culture increasingly dominates America, as the plastic dining experience creeps across our exurbs and into our cities, it only makes adult restaurants put up more defenses and become more adult. The divide grows.

There's a particular expression I've noticed on the faces of parents when they eat out with their family. It's one of waiting. They're resigned, giving this dinner as a bribe to their children so that at some later date they can run off to someplace on their own. It's an expression of defeat, an acknowledgment that the children have won. In its way it is decidedly un-American, as the family has been split.

In the twelve years Elise and I have been together we've spent much of it looking at each other over a table. We will continue to eat out alone. But as with travel, a stubborn part of me wants as much as possible to eat out as a family. I want my children drawing on the tablecloth and playing under the table, but eventually coming up and drinking watered-down wine and being a part of the art of eating.

My argumentative French friend told me about the Danish word *hygge*. *Hygge* has no English equivalent. It describes what occurs after dinner, after a few bottles of wine, when good friends are drinking coffee and appreciating each other's beautiful if accentuated qualities to the point that the evening glows and the world becomes wonderful. *Hygge* is that space. A certain sweetness, fed by food and time and the care we bring to it. And how can a dinner be *hygge* if we are eating mac and cheese under fluorescent lights in a plastic booth in some family restaurant on the outskirts of town?

I've been eating out alone the last two days. Elise had a psychology conference back East and since the breast milk was going, Zoë went, too. When I picked them up at the airport I was amazed at how much heavier one of them had become. Zoë was more animated, too. On our way home we stopped at a diner in Oakland. Zoë bashed the menu with her fist, eyes wide as she stared at it upside down. We ordered burgers and fries. She ripped napkins and the table started to look like the day after a parade, and then the food came. She ate avocado. She grabbed fries. She grabbed ketchup. She grabbed our hair.

Elise and I took turns eating, and walking with Zoë. I walked her to the kitchen where we watched the cook flip burgers, then outside where we looked at a dog tied to a parking meter. We returned and Zoë nursed—smearing avocado over Elise's shirt—and Elise and I were able, briefly, to look at each other and talk about the trip. Half an hour later we were done. As Elise packed to go, I crawled under the table to clean up the fries that were lying there like branches after a windstorm, and while I was reaching for one behind the table leg, I hit my head. Hard, on top where it hurts. I put my hand to my head and took it away and it was covered in blood. No, ketchup. This was pathetic. I got the sense, as I squatted on my hands and knees under the table with ketchup in my hair and fries in my hands, that we were hanging on. That eating out with Zoë would become only more difficult, and then something else, and that this chapter was far from over.

—the snot-suction thing—

It's snowing when our plane touches down in Washington, D.C. Christmas morning, cold and dark. The terminal doors slide open and we are hit with a blast of bitter air. We bundle the girl in blankets and she stares through the car windows at the falling flakes of snow. The wipers beat back and forth and the tires hiss through the slush as we pass through an ice-crusted expanse of overpasses and parking lots. Everything feels depressed, not well. It's as if the entire East Coast is a contiguous gray highway. We're not in California anymore.

This is Zoë's first extended trip. She'll be introduced to snow and cold, to new beds, to new people. Fourteen days of unfamiliarity and family. What were we thinking?

When we pull up to Elise's brother's house in D.C., I sit in the car for a moment and think, *Let's keep driving*. Then the front door of the house opens and the relatives are on us. Actually, they're on Zoë, hugging and kissing and squeezing her. Zoë's cousins are sick. They're little faucets of phlegm. The boy cousin holds Zoë by the ears and sneezes. Then he coughs. Then someone tells him to cover his mouth and he does, and coughs and wipes his hand on her head. Zoë just sits and stares. In fact, she's in love. I love her cousins, too, though I'd like them better now if they were wrapped in plastic.

Zoë gets loads of gifts. The house is wall-to-wall wrapping paper and family. The family cat has gone into hiding. I'm hiding behind a book. I look over at Zoë and see that her cousin is exploring her nose with his tongue. That can't be good. We should go for a walk. So I wrap Zoë in a snowsuit that makes her look like a yeti and we head out into the searing cold and come back in ten minutes. She naps with her face buried in a blanket.

After two days we cram with Elise's parents into a car and drive north. We stop in Brooklyn, and visit Elise's grandmother. Zoë is fascinated by her great-grandmother's squeaky voice and amazed when her great-grandmother grabs her ears and drags her in for a mouth-to-mouth kiss. After lunch, after another mouth-to-mouth kiss, we head into Manhattan.

We're on our own, finally. We spend the day in the Village hopping from café to café, searching for hot chocolate and a comfortable place to breast-feed. The first café has weak hot chocolate and hard wooden seats. The next café has hot chocolate you can stand your spoon in but only stools to sit on. We settle at Doma, a café with cozy seats and wide windows looking out on Seventh Avenue. The woman next to us gushes over Zoë. Elise whispers, "She looks like Hilary Swank's sister." It is Hilary Swank. She's playing chess with her husband, and Zoë spends the afternoon tossing her toy under their table and they keep picking it up and giving it back. We spend the afternoon reading books and ignoring the fact that we recognize Hilary Swank. The only problem with Doma is its coffee, a problem for a café, which combines being bad with being expensive.

We spend the next day in more cafés drinking more hot chocolate. Occasionally we bundle up for a walk in the cold. Once we see Sarah Jessica Parker walking down the other side of the street with her baby in her Baby Björn and she waves at us and we wave at her before diving back into a café.

Night comes. Zoë's nose was already running but now it's sprinting. She sleeps fitfully, can't breathe. We hear her wheezing on the makeshift bed of cushions we've set up next to our bed in the apartment where we're staying. It sounds as if she's trying to drag the last bits of a milk shake through a straw. By midnight her nose is completely clogged. We get out The Snot-Suction Thing.

The Snot-Suction Thing looks like an onion with a nose. Its light-blue color could be called *Hospital Sick*. It is medieval, emphasis on "eval." But when we shove its nose up Zoë's nose, and release the onion, The Snot-Suction Thing yanks out a satisfying sinewy strand of goo. Zoë feels better and sleeps, at least for the hour until we de-snot her again. During the night, "de-snot" becomes a verb.

In the morning we take five minutes cleaning up the wadded tissues covering the floor. Then we slog out into the cold to visit friends uptown. Zoë is exhausted. We're not feeling too great either. We make a bed for Zoë on our friend's bed and she sleeps, then we head downtown and set up another bed at another friend's house and she sleeps again. As we talk with our friends in the living room we want nothing more than to lounge around and catch up on gossip. But we have become nervous on-call plumbers, one of our ears always tuned to the gurgling from the other room, which at some point will burst into a full-on pipe malfunction that requires our services, our little baby plunger.

We retreat to New Haven, wads of tissues crammed in every pocket. My parents live outside of town on a farm. We spend New Year's Eve playing charades and pumping snot out of Zoë and wondering how many pints of snot can be in one baby's head.

Elise has an interview the next day for her predoctoral internship. While she's gone I wrap Zoë in a blanket and walk around the farm, kicking snow into the air and onto the backs of my parents' dogs. It's odd to show Zoë where I grew up and it moves me in a way I can't quite describe— she's in a place where she never existed, but was always part of the future story. She's nowhere but everywhere. We return home and Zoë naps, snoring like a phlegmatic old man.

The Snot-Suction Thing is clogged. It needs a suction of its own. Should I use a turkey baster on it? A turkey baster on my daughter? This is getting ridiculous. In the morning we bundle Zoë and drive up another slushy highway to visit my brother. He and his wife own the general store in a small Massachusetts town. They live above the store and treat it like a pantry, walking down for pints of Ben & Jerry's whenever they want. I like visiting. But this year I'm walking downstairs to see if the store kitchen has a turkey baster. Zoë may not need anything, though. She's getting better. Nursing has literally nursed her back to health. Her face is an ugly record of the ten days she's been through: raw and red and covered with dried mucus that sticks to her skin like yellow lichen on a slick rock. She sleeps through the night. In the morning her snots are hard and I can shovel them out of her nose with the tip of my pinky. I don't bother with tissues anymore and am wiping the snots on my socks.

Our last stop is in Boston. When Elise goes to another internship interview I stay with Zoë at a friend's apartment. Another futon, another temporary bed, another pile of dirty clothes and winter jackets. Being in yet another place that is not ours makes me wish that I could pack an entire warm room in my shoulder bag, with Zoë's bed and clothes arranged neatly inside. It would fold easily in and out, and if I could pack my child in the bag, too, and ensure that she was never sick, travel would be so easy.

Zoë naps and I sit in the kitchen and nurse a coffee and listen to the radio. A man is talking about how his baby got ill and died in her crib so I go check on Zoë. She is flat on her back, immune to her surroundings, breathing easy after all she's been through. I guess The Snot-Suction Thing did its job. It expired in the process, though. It's broken, like us.

I return to the kitchen and put my head on the table. Outside, through windows fogged with cold, I hear the crunch of boots in snow, the swish of car wheels through slush, the occasional clatter of falling icicles. Inside I hear the asthmatic rattle of the radiator. I close my eyes and picture the produce section of Berkeley Bowl. I picture the tomatoes. I picture tomatoes that are a certain red that is rich and bursting to the point of being so full of color that you can't imagine a deeper color in the world, where if you put your hands on them you can sense the soil they came from and the sun they must have grown under. I picture the leeks and the radishes, dripping wet. Each color distinct and sharp. And as I daydream my bag full of produce and walk outside into the sun and look up at the hills and smell that bright clean smell that is distinctly California, I want to go home. I want to go home to our home three thousand miles away.

—a chair no baby could possibly fall out of—

I've spilled soup on Zoë, poked her in the eye with a fork, covered her nose in newsprint when I was trying to get out snot, thrown a Frisbee with her in my arms and given her whiplash, flipped her over in the jogger, and kicked a soccer ball into her head.

But I have not dropped her. Not yet. I am increasingly preoccupied with when the drop will be. The longer I go without it happening the more inevitable it seems. I'm like a shortstop who hasn't made an error all season, which just means that the bad-hop grounder that will break his streak is going to happen at some point, and more likely sooner than later. The tension is getting to me. When I played baseball in high school the worst part was tensing before every pitch. Then, nothing happened. And nothing happened all afternoon except for three split-second moments when the baseball would come screaming out to me in center field and I'd have to race off and try to catch it. It's the same with Zoë. She'll be safe for hours and then, like a ball jumping off a bat, try to leap onto the stove.

The boredom and suddenness of baseball was one of the reasons I liked football better. I wanted the ball in my hands. In college I was a receiver, and though I wasn't big or strong, I didn't drop the ball. Because of this, when I came into the dining hall after practice my friends would throw food at me. They thought this was funny. And of course, I'd drop the loaf of bread or the banana or whatever they threw at me and spend the next hour begging them to throw more food. So while I think I have good hands, when I hold Zoë I'm not so sure. I'm fooled by her odd shape, her slipperiness, her lack of laces. And a football isn't a baby. Babies don't bounce.

It's winter, and the rainy season is here. The place to be is Royal Coffee ensconced in a comfy chair with a coffee and a book looking out at the weather through the big glass windows. Royal is on College Avenue, just across the Oakland border. It's on a corner. Outside are metal tables, an awning, a red metal clock that doesn't work. Inside is a hissing espresso machine, a blackboard with the day's coffee written in chalk, a few tables, three red leather chairs. It's a small, somewhat clean, well-lighted place which also serves the strongest coffee in the Bay Area.

A good café is like the big rock in the big pool of a slow-moving river. Bugs and beetles and broken branches come floating by, then get caught in the back current and whirling eddies and stay awhile. Constant movement, going nowhere. I like to think I'm a trout holding next to that rock, watching nature swirl around me. Before Zoë was born, I came to Royal every afternoon, to look over my work, to read, and to watch people. Now I want Zoë to be part of my café life. The red leather chairs will be safe for her to sit in, I think. They are wide and round and deep. The elbow of the chair is almost concave and that is where I will put her. We will walk to Royal in the rain and sit together in the big safe red leather chairs and look out the windows as the world floats past. That's the idea, at least.

The regulars at Royal are bikers. They come in two colors. There are bikers in pink, Lycra-clad cyclists who sit outside and sip organic fair-trade coffee and rearrange their balls before clicking into racing bikes and gliding slowly up into the Oakland hills. And there are bikers in black, motorcyclists with EAST BAY RATS insignia sewn on leather jackets who buy their Celebes Kalosi (no milk, sugar) and sit outside and spread their chaps wide and rearrange their balls and stroke their well-groomed facial hair and talk about their new carburetor before roaring up into the Oakland hills. There are other Royal regulars, too: the woman with the parrots, the dot-comers with funky glasses and fancy shoes, the initially sane-sounding crazies who tell anyone sitting next to them what really went down with George W. Bush, the C.I.A., and their mother.

The regulars make Royal a good place not only to watch people, but also to eavesdrop. Stories, heard over the course of weeks and months, evolve in installments: the confrontation with the landlord, the court case involving the crash with the garage, the recent threeway. The stories often end with the declaration that the narrator will lay into so-and-so's ass, right after they finish drinking their latte. I listened one afternoon to a man commiserating with friends because his fiancée left him that morning, the day of their wedding. "Dude, that's *harsh*!" his friends said, nodding and looking up at clouds over the Oakland hills. "And on such a sweet day!"

The view of the Oakland hills from Royal Coffee *is* sweet. The hills rise above the Safeway across the street in muscley shadows. Stucco houses dot their flanks and when the afternoon light strikes at a certain angle one red house turns pink. At the end of the day commuters walk from the BART along College Avenue and pick through produce in the green market on 63rd Street. They wait in line at the flower stand. Couples meet. A bearded panhandler greets everyone from a director's chair. The same two pigeons, it seems, sit on top of the orange "S" of the Safeway sign and have sex. Traffic stops and starts. In the crosswalk there are often confrontations between pedestrians and drivers. Buses run into things. Once I saw a woman fall over a speed bump, then get up, and walk backward, and fall over the speed bump again. Overseeing the whole scene are the Royal workers. The workers are mean, which I find comforting. They make snide comments about customers after they leave and I can only guess what they say about me. They like Zoë, though.

As we walk through the door, and fold our umbrella, the Royal workers give her a big smile. The worker with the ear studs makes my coffee while the one with the lip rings squeezes Zoë's cheek. I take off our raincoats and set up one of the red leather chairs. Then I get my coffee and slide Zoë far back into the chair so there is no way she can fall out, none. We sit and wait for friends to come and watch people walk past through the foggy windows and I whisper: "That biker has a hole in his pants. That biker is flipping off the bus driver. That woman is about to trip over the speed bump."

When Zoë did fall, off the rocking chair at home, it wasn't so bad. She was playing with a rattle and tossing it off the edge and I was absentmindedly retrieving it for her. My back was turned. I was watching a football game on television. Elise was writing at her desk. At some point the rattle went off the rocker and I didn't hear it and I guess Zoë leaned and kept leaning and the rocking chair leaned, too, and I heard Elise shout from across the room and felt movement behind me and out of the corner of my eye saw a falling ball of pink pants. I dove, my hands reaching out for her, and in that moment it seemed I was twenty years old, playing football again, coming out of my break on the practice fields at Yale and turning to see the ball spiraling toward me as time slowed and noise shut down and the only two things that existed in the entire world were me and the ball, my hands reaching out to bring it into my arms, a single moment of concentration and calm before the defender and the grass beneath me made their presence known, and life began again. As I think about it, it would have been a great catch. Zoë went into my hands, and then through them, and hit the floor with a thump. She didn't cry right away. It took a minute until the shock of her downward trajectory caught up with her, and then it sounded like she'd been plugged into an electrical outlet. Elise held and nursed her. She was fine, if a bit addled, and when I try to put a good spin on this, she learned that it's not a good idea to leap off high places.

As we sit in the red leather chairs at Royal Coffee now, we are watching the world float past outside the fogged windows. Elise comes, friends come. Our table piles with mugs. We talk about what we did that day and Zoë fumbles with a spoon and we while away the afternoon, a relaxed rainy winter day inside a warm café. Even so, I keep one hand on Zoë's back and the other one poised to catch her. I still have not dropped her. But I have not caught her, and am waiting for a second chance. I'm waiting for the next play. Though if my hands are not steady I have the feeling she will survive no matter what I do. That if I do drop her, when I do drop her, it is likely she will land on something soft.

—ha ha ha—

Not long ago, after months of backseat babysitting, Elise and I started sitting together in the front seat of the car again. We felt a bit secretive. When Zoë was looking the other way I'd jump out of the back and come in the front, sliding in and resting my hand on Elise's knee. It was like we were in middle school, surreptitiously stealing a moment from the chaperone who didn't want us holding hands.

Elise and I also started dating again. At night, after we put Zoë to sleep, a friend would come over and sit on the couch and we would leave. We'd walk to the car in the dark—teenagers now creeping out our bedroom windows—and sit for a moment in the quiet, filled with worry, thrilled to be alone.

Our first time we went to César, a trendy bar in the shade of Chez Panisse. It has low lighting and high prices, a drink menu a foot long. The customers are single or single-acting. It's the place that people in Berkeley go to when they wish they lived in New York. It stays open past nine. I don't know differences between wines, have no idea what makes up a martini, but we found ourselves ordering cocktails with names like Andalusian Sidecars. This was an absurd way to remind ourselves we were a couple, and it was hard to forget we had a child because for the first half hour she was all we talked about. "Do you think she's okay?" I said. "Did you see the funny thing she did today?" said Elise. Eventually we talked about other things, and then it was time to go. We drove home, sitting in the car outside for one last moment.

Our desire to be with each other is complicated by Zoë's desire that we never leave. Well, I can leave. Elise can't. Zoë is increasingly aware of exactly where Elise is. If Elise walks to the kitchen, Zoë's eyes follow her as if she's leaving her on an island. Zoë likes me, but needs Elise. Elise said, "Zoë would most like to be held by me while looking at you." But I'm not sure Zoë wouldn't mind being held by Elise and looking at her, too.

I wouldn't mind being held by Elise. The problem with Zoë's wanting Elise more is I want Elise more, too. And while this opens up a host of odd questions, and while I don't want to think I'm competing with my daughter for my wife's affection, it is true that I am getting obsessed with Elise's breasts.

I've always liked them. Now I *like* them. I'm looking at them more than at Elise. I'm aware that she doesn't exactly appreciate my appreciation since now there are two people in the house fixated on when next she's going to take off her shirt. The terrible thing is that it hurts Elise when I touch her breasts too hard, and since this means her breasts are frequently off-limits, I have become, through deprivation, that much more hungry. It's like a friend dropped off two rich chocolate cakes at my house and asked me to keep them in the fridge and look after them for a couple of months.

Elise likened sex after giving birth to a ring of fire, which can't have been good. It's getting better, though, maybe even lip-bitingly better than before. It could be because finding the time for sex is a delicious obstacle, or it could be that we're trying to be quiet with a sleeping baby nearby. Whatever the reasons, as soon as Zoë goes down for her nap I'm dragging Elise to bed.

Unfortunately, it turns out that Zoë has serious comic timing. When things start stirring in our bed, she starts crying in hers. She has interrupted us countless times, during the most inopportune and exciting moments. We can't escape Zoë unless we go out to the car and have sex in the backseat. She's always *there*.

My fantasy recently is finding time alone with Elise. Not just for sex, but for walking down a street and holding hands or reading in a café with our feet in each other's laps. Slow meaningless together time. The problem of having our time alone be so rare is that once we find it we're so wound up we're verbally undressing each other. It's like we've never met. And yet, we have to go through this rushed stripping and fumbling before we can reach a place where we can be quiet with each other, naked. Then, in that nonverbal almost postcoital space, we connect again as a couple.

I want to make sure Elise and I always find the time *not* to talk with each other. Or, if we must, to talk about trivial things. We enjoy talking about Zoë so much that I fear, in seventeen years, when she leaves, we'll have nothing to say. I don't want to be a couple that has forgotten both how to speak and how to be silent with each other. With Zoë increasingly inserted between us, what will happen when she's no longer there?

Last week, after another afternoon of comically inter-rupted sex, Zoë came to bed and was playing a game with Elise that made no sense to me. Something about raising a leg and pushing it down. I was lying there frustrated but Elise and Zoë were looking into each other's eyes like the oldest of friends and giggling hysterically, laughing because they were laughing. Ha ha ha.

That night I was grumpy. I was eating dinner and staring at Elise's breasts. Zoë was staring at Elise's breasts, too, waggling her hands excitedly. "Hey Zoë," I said. "How about some milk and cookies? But, without the cookies!" This is a line Elise and I have repeated fifty times. I read somewhere that a joke is funny for the first three times you hear it, not so funny from the fourth to the seventh time, and then hilarious.

As Zoë found the breast and her face relaxed into blissful happiness, Elise and I looked at each other and cracked up. Zoë gives us so much to laugh at, from her goofy expressions to our little jokes. She entangles our lives, turning tragedy to comedy. When I am frustrated that I can't be with Elise at least I can joke about it. Laughing keeps me from exploding, I guess. Through laughing I am able to see that things are not so dire. That Elise and I will be together again, that our time will come.

As I sat there, watching Zoë with the breasts I wanted to be with, I realized that I cared that Zoë has a sense of humor more than any other sense. I don't care if she's good in school or sports, don't care if she's nice or wants to save the world. But if she can laugh at the world, then it is hers.

———

She will need a sense of humor if we move to Chicago. Elise is applying for a predoctoral internship at the University of Illinois at Chicago. In January we fly there for the interview. We touch down at O'Hare. Everything is flat and gray and freezing. Steam pouring out of grates onto grimy streets. Elise heads to the interview and Zoë and I head to the nearest warm place with warm drinks. When she gets tired I bundle her in the car and she sleeps. We drive through neighborhoods: Pilsen, Ukrainian Village, South Side. I drive up along frozen Lake Michigan and circle drafty deserted Wrigley Field. Seeing it makes me dream of blue skies and summer and day games. The siren of a fire truck jolts me out of my daydream and I three-point and speed the other way, checking the still-sleeping girl in the rearview. All of Chicago seems to be on fire today, or all its cats stuck in trees, because I spend the next hour trying to drive in the opposite direction of fire trucks. Zoë is finally woken by an ambulance siren that erupts next to us.

After picking up Elise we go to a café in Wicker Park called Earwax. It's warm inside, like an ear. We shed layers and talk about her interview, our fire trucks, the possibility of moving to Chicago. As our clothes come off we begin to seriously think about moving here. Why not? It's different, the opposite of Berkeley. Elise and I start getting excited, making plans, imagining our way into the future. We look outside—a lone trash bag is hopping in gusts down Milwaukee Avenue—and we groan at the shock of possibly living here. "*Chicago!*" we repeat, eyes wide as if someone were pouring a bucket of ice water on our heads and we liked it.

The next day is even colder, zero degrees. We pull Zoë's hat low over her eyes. It's a red hat with a knob on top that makes her look like a cardinal, especially today when she's wearing a long black dress. It's funny to see our young girl looking like an old man. On the flight back to California that afternoon, sitting a few rows in front of us is another old man, the former special prosecutor and sex investigator Ken Starr. He's taking notes on a yellow legal pad. Every time I walk Zoë up and down the aisle, Starr looks up from his writing and does this creepy little wagging-finger wave right in Zoë's face, like he's giving a mouse an erotic massage. It's the Ken Starr Wave now, permanently affixed in my mind. I walk back and tell Elise, and she laughs and I put my arm around her and give her a kiss, almost unaware of the baby between us.

—that's a sheep, that's a goat—

My older brother and I both have chin dimples. The similarities end there. He's handsome. He has tight, curly blond hair and looks like the guy in those old Camel cigarette billboard ads. He's as talkative as a billboard, too. When we did chores together in our barn growing up, the only sounds were the swishing of the horses' tails and me babbling about something. My brother works with horses now, building cross-country courses for a living. The closest I come to horses is when I draw them in a book. But animals are in my blood.

I worry Zoë won't know animals. We read her books filled with pigs and sheep, and have a herd of stuffed cows lying around the house, but what is a cow if you've never seen a real one? Is it a foot-tall black-and-white fuzzy thing that moos when you squeeze its middle? Last fall we drove to farms in nearby Orinda to show Zoë the real thing. I wanted especially for her to see pigs: their bristly backs, low grunts, intelligent eyes. Coming around a bend I saw a farm with a corral full of pigs. "Pigs!" I yelled. But Zoë was sleeping. "*Wake up. Pigs!*" I whispered. I drove away without her seeing anything.

Even the animals we had had at my family's farm in Connecticut were long gone. When we stayed there over the holidays, I told Zoë stories instead. I told her how I'd walk to the barn in the morning to milk the goats, or how I'd forget to shut the gate and all the cows would get out. But these were just words.

When we came home I brought Zoë to the Oakland Zoo. "You're going to see a tiger!" I said. But when we reached the tiger cage, the tiger was sleeping and Zoë was watching a scrap of paper blowing in the wind. At the lion den the lions were napping in high grass and Zoë was exploring my ear. At the giraffe pen the giraffes were standing still as trees and Zoë was more interested in a flock of pigeons. All the animals at the zoo were motionless. We might as well have been looking at pictures.

Finally, two weeks ago, I took Zoë over the hills to Tilden Park and the Little Farm. I'd only recently heard of it. As the name says, it's not large. A cluster of sheds and pens, a windmill turning above a red barn, all tucked into the shade of a grove of eucalyptus trees. Despite its size, the Little Farm is a big discovery. Walking toward it the first time, I heard the lowing of a cow and a feeling welled inside me that I can only describe as exhilaration. The animals were here! All the animals I'd been inanely imitating for months! And they were awake! There were geese honking over lettuce and humping each other, sheep rubbing against a fence, goats bleating, cows chewing their cud, pigs slopping in mud, chickens squawking. Zoë's eyes popped. The geese made her laugh out loud. She tried to grab the rams' wool. Only the goats got no response from her, which made me sad, as I love goats. But I drove home from the Little Farm elated, and that night Zoë had her first taste of chicken, which seemed fitting.

It's a good time to go to the Little Farm. The winter rains have ended. The hills are green and there's a feel of spring in the air, a sense of buds opening up. After going to the farm, Zoë and I sit in the sun and eat a snack and look through one of her animal picture books, pointing out the ones we just saw. The book makes sense, the farm makes sense.

We go every few days now. Zoë still prefers the horny geese and the woolly sheep. She likes touching the cows' wet noses. She's warming to the goats. But I'm getting fed up with the Berkeley parents misidentifying the animals. The parents look bored to begin with—taking their children to the farm because one is supposed to take one's children to the farm. And they talk in a voice just loud enough so that everyone nearby knows that what is being said is educational and child-appropriate. I *despise* that voice.

"Hey Sierra, look at the pretty sheep!" one mother says, pointing at a goat.

"Hey Sierra, *share* your greens with the nice duck!" the mother continues, gesturing at a thirty-pound goose. I walk away with Zoë to the ram pen. Sierra and her mother follow and we stand against the fence.

"Hey Sierra, pet the nice sheep. Isn't she a pretty sheep?!" Ram, *ram!* I mutter to myself. Sierra pats the nice animal anyway, his eyes bulging and rolling back in contentment as his knobbly knees knock into his testicles.

As I look at the ram I think about my brother, and not because of their similar hair and reserved nature. Because I bet he'd be looking at this Berkeley mother in the same way I am. He wouldn't say anything; maybe he'd flare his nostrils. But he'd be thinking what I am. Not only that this woman is an idiot but that there is a respectful way to approach animals. It's judgmental, and it comes from our farm upbringing. Growing up together shaped us in at least one similar way, even as we moved in different directions. It surprises me to realize my brother and I share anything, a common "experiential gene," and it makes me think about the ways I try to shape Zoë.

I kick balls with her, I read books to her, I let her play with my paints. If pressed I would admit that I'd like it if Zoë liked sports and writing and art. Once I admit this I back off and say that all I care about is that she is happy. Then I back off that, too, as happiness is a lot to ask of anybody. It's hard, though, not to want your child to love what you love.

When I was ten my mother gave me a set of watercolors, the same set I use now. When I was ten my parents never encouraged me to play sports, and I played all the time, and still do. So how do you look back and determine what a parent's influence has been? You can't completely. How do you look forward and guess what a parent's influence will be? You don't. It's a poor game, predicting the unpredictable.

In the face of this uncertainty I make jokes as usual. I tell Elise that, since Zoë will probably act out against whatever we do, we should be clever and subvert this and enroll Zoë in our local chapter of the John Birch Society and get her a gun *now*.

These are absurd thoughts to have about a girl not yet one year old, I know. It's presumptuous to think my daughter's interests will be formed only because of, or in spite of, me. Maybe that's the point, though. Being a parent is all irrational anxiety. Am I showing her the right things, keeping her from the wrong things? Am I showing her too much? Not enough? Most anxiety-producing of all, am I neglecting to show her one particular thing that she would have fallen head over heels in love with, and by this omission, will I let her down forever? Am I not providing for my child and don't even know it?

I'm beginning to understand the parental desire to give the world to one's child and the anxiety that comes when you realize you cannot. I can't believe, in moments like this, that I empathize with the Berkeley parents who are bringing their children to the Little Farm, but I do.

Elise and I say we will expose Zoë to the things in the world we love. We will take her to soccer practice or dance rehearsal. I will give her watercolors and try to remember to encourage her in chemistry. I may even get her a BB gun. We will lead her to what we hope are green pastures even as we try to support wherever the flight of her interests takes her. That's what we tell ourselves. I know my intentions with Zoë will miss their mark or be misconstrued and taken in a way I never thought imaginable. I have no answers. I bring her to animals.

After saying goodbye to the rams we walk back to the geese, who are having a raucous bout of goose sex in the pool. Sierra's mother knows what's going on. "Hey Sierra, say bye-bye to the ducks and let's go see the *pigs*!" She's right, for once, about the pigs. Sometimes I wonder if nothing, nothing at all matters when raising one's children. Sierra will grow up confused about sheep, and so what? Zoë will grow up confused about what I am not even sure. She will love what she loves. The last time we went to the farm, Zoë's favorite animal was the windmill.

—almost april—

It's almost April. The Berkeley hills are warm with the smell of wisteria and lavender, alive with the buzz of garden clippers. Our tall windows are open again and we can hear the neighbor across the creek playing the piano. The opera singer has moved and a bagpiper has taken her place, which is amusing for a day. Hummingbirds are everywhere and one flies into our apartment and we spend an hour with a broom and a bucket trying to coax it to safety and I finally pin it against the wall and release it outside only to see that I inadvertently removed its tail feathers. I killed a hummingbird. But even this cannot diminish my happiness that the world is blossoming all around us. In fact, it has the odd effect of increasing it. Hummingbirds are here. Spring is here!

Elise and I had been thinking it was time for Zoë to meet more babies. As it was, whenever she encountered someone her own size her eyes would go wide and she'd dive back into our arms. So a few weeks ago I took her to our local playground. It's in Codornices Park. I walked there down steep steps through a redwood grove. A creek tumbled beside us and as we got closer I could see a concrete slide snaking under an oak tree. Children flew down the slide on flattened cardboard and the rubbing sound was constant, as if the park itself had fat thighs and was wearing corduroy. Next to the slide was the playground, packed with swings and slides and sand. Below the playground was the Berkeley Rose Garden, full of roses on trellises and gravelly paths and shadowed wooden benches. This was sure to be fertile ground for meeting babies.

But when I got to the playground I felt like a matchmaker, or a pimp. There I was, sitting in the sand, checking out everyone who walked by and holding up my daughter to see if there were any takers, anybody who would come over and give her a good time. But no one was buying, or selling. I was missing something in the baby pimping game.

I kept coming, though. After a few days of watching the

other parents I realized the playground was like a bar. There were accepted and equally choreographed opening lines: "How old is your baby?" "Is she crawling yet?" "What a pretty hat!" (said if the baby is ugly). All was code. This should have been obvious, though I never was comfortable in bars.

I found my own opener. I started bringing a soccer ball. I dribbled it down the steps and because I had no skill, kicked it into the creek. After fishing it out I sat with Zoë in the playground and poured sand over the ball and the other babies circled like pigeons around crumbs: poking, picking, bobbing their heads. The parents followed the babies, we said our lines, and we gathered around our children as they began to play. Hookup accomplished, with maybe a phone number to come.

From my lap, Zoë stared at the other babies as they grabbed the ball and then each other's noses. Afterward I'd walk to the Rose Garden, and Zoë, quiet and watchful a minute before, would babble madly as if describing what she had seen. I kicked the ball in front of us and sometimes I'd swing Zoë way back like a croquet mallet, and have her touch the ball lightly while kicking it hard myself and she'd crack up. At the Rose Garden, Zoë would pick the head off a rose and I'd look around to see if anyone noticed. Then we'd walk home, stopping at bushes on the way to pluck berries which stayed clutched in her fingers until she gave them, along with the crumpled rose, to Elise.

Walking to Codornices Park one morning we saw our neighbor's cat and Zoë grabbed its tail. When we got to the playground she sat in the sand and when a baby boy was brought to us, she reached out and grabbed his hat. She started grabbing all the kids' hats. The drooling twins, the girl with the tofu snacks, the boy with the same sunglasses as his mother, the countless kids named Sequoia. Nobody's hat was safe. In the next week I spent a lot of time apologizing and prying sun hats out of Zoë's surprisingly strong fingers. Often I didn't know to whom I was apologizing. The Sequoias seemed to have multiple caregivers and the code says baby names are known and parent names are not. Was this Sequoia's mother, her nanny, one of her lesbian parents? It made for interesting guesswork. As Zoë went to the park with Elise, too, the same confusion could be said of us. Zoë was the constant: *the girl who grabs hats.*

Since she was stealing hats I thought it would be good for her to learn to get away with it. It's not effective stealing if you take something and just sit there. She needed to learn to run, or at least crawl. And she needed new marks. We started heading south of campus to Willard Park. Willard had a bigger playground, a sandlot with toys, and a rubber surface on which toddlers and toddlers-to-be could bounce.

Around the park were sequoias—the trees—through which one could see wood-shingled houses, the concrete buildings of campus, and the Oakland hills where, if squinting, one could see the speck of a hiker or the white spread of a flock of brush-eating goats.

Zoë sat and stared at the toddlers. She fell for a boy with tousled blond hair. As he wobbled past she reached up at him with one hand, pounded the rubber with the other, and rolled onto her back. Sometimes I gave my fingers to Zoë and hovered over her as she stumbled around like a drunk. Often I sat and talked with other parents and let her flail on her own, only righting her when she got stuck on her back like a turtle.

The parents' favorite subject was how little they were sleeping. The rest of us would nod our heads sympathetically and think, "Thank God my baby isn't getting up at three!" (Schadenfreude is parenting's unspoken language.) Once a mother from Marin looked at me with big concerned eyes and catalogued all the things that were dangerous for her daughter to eat—peanut butter, apples, wheat—and all the careful steps she was taking to prevent anything bad from happening—consulting her pediatrician weekly, reading the right books, maintaining constant vigilance—and couldn't see that her daughter was sitting behind her eating sand. Another mother, terrified that her daughter would choke on Cheerios, had been cutting them into quarters, but lightened up recently after realizing that maybe she was being a bit overly protective and was now only cutting the Cheerios into halves.

I shouldn't feel good about other parents' anxieties, as I have my own. I worry a dog will bite Zoë. Zoë loves dogs. There's a grass area next to the playground where dogs run off leash. I take Zoë there after playing and she whirls her arms with excitement at all the barking and ball-chasing. She wants to grab the dogs. She is fearless around them.

Playgrounds have become my new habitat. My shoulder bag, which always had a sketchbook, now has a diaper and a hat and a snack. I've learned to find the swing in the shade, to test metal slides and see if they're hot. I've learned how to put sunblock on Zoë's nose with one hand while putting her sun hat on with the other. I've learned, without thinking, to lift Zoë's rear to my nose to check her diaper. And I do all this with something approaching naturalness. I even know how to approach parents in the playground and make small talk, though I haven't learned how not to tell stories about them later.

At night my sneakers are full of sand. Zoë's shoes are full of sand, too, and there is sand in every crevice of her body. When we bathe her she splashes the water and her hands shake she's so tired from her day. Then Elise reads her

Goodnight Moon and she reaches out and helps turn the pages, her eyebrows rising with each new one.

In the spring after we moved to California, something odd happened. I was painting at my desk and the front door was open and after a while I got the sense that somebody was very close and staring at me. I turned, and there at my feet, looking up at me with its head turned to one side, was a baby deer. She had quietly walked into our house and up to my desk. "Hey," I said, and then louder as I realized I shouldn't encourage this behavior. She turned, batted her tail at me, and click-clacked across the parquet floor and out the door to the garden. I can still see her looking up at me with those big eyes. Inquisitive, nervy, a little dumb. She was poking her nose into things, even if that meant exploring inside a house. And just as this deer was curious of the inside, Zoë is curious of everything outside. She's the baby deer in reverse. She's reaching into the world, into a wild place of sand and swings and dogs and other children whose hats she can take, lightly holding our hands as she stumbles forward.

—a place at the table, second course—

The popular sushi place in Berkeley is Kirala. It's in a ware-house near campus with large glass windows. Lines form at five, and soon the place is packed with mousse-haired couples talking under the designy blue lights that hang over the counter. Special rolls come like caterpillars, with watercress antennae. Sometimes Elise and I go to Kirala; more often we go to a place in a Korean supermarket in Oakland called Koryo. Koryo has five tables, and good cheap sushi. We've gotten to know the owner and his wife. When she was pregnant we tracked the growth of her belly and when Elise was pregnant they did the same. The owner makes a special roll when I ask. Koryo is the place we go without thinking, a place where you can take your time, and a place where you can be gone in thirty minutes.

Thirty minutes is important because we're on a timer this spring. The infinitely charming, occasionally active handbag we had in the fall has become an infinitely active, occasionally charming handbag that may soon explode. Zoë is a dining time bomb; thirty minutes is how long she lasts before detonation. We've been going to Koryo a lot lately. We order, Zoë plays with the menu, I take her to the bathroom and we play with the singing plastic carp on the wall, we return, eat, and leave in twenty-nine minutes.

But if we're out with friends we have to last longer than half an hour, often with volatile results. Last month we went to a trendy French restaurant in San Francisco complete with a waiter with a possibly fake French accent. The tables were close, the noisy conversation of other diners closer. Zoë nursed through most of dinner out of shock. When she came up for air she threw a wine glass. We'd brought an avocado and shoved pieces into her mouth, adding what she didn't eat to our salads. We juggled toys, played with spoons, went for walks. It wasn't relaxing. Our ears were bent toward both Zoë and our friends, not able to understand either. The only person we were able to understand was the waiter, that he was full of it. Zoë exploded in the restaurant and then on the Bay Bridge and all the way home.

Sometimes we forget we have this bomb and attempt to go someplace we went before Zoë was with us. Last year we found a sushi place in San Francisco, a hole in the wall, with no sign saying it's a restaurant besides the row of sake bottles in the window. We should have known better than to go there with a baby. It's the type of place where the only sound you can hear is other people chewing. But the old couple who run it have always been friendly to us. This time they mumbled when they saw us walk in with Zoë. They raised their eyebrows when they saw us take a toy out of our bag. They frowned when Elise showed Zoë the sake bottles. They glared when Zoë cried for a moment, which she did when she ate rice which had been, unknowingly, at least to us, smeared with wasabi. They were all smiles when they brought the check early.

To avoid incidents like this, we've been planning differently. We were already going out on Monday or Tuesday to avoid crowds; now we're eating out in the afternoon. When no other customers are around, when a place has just opened and the waiters are cleaning up from their own meal.

Last month we went to a small Italian restaurant in San

Francisco. The sun was shining. We sat at a booth in the window and ordered a pizza. As we waited for our food, Zoë ate olives. She sipped some of my wine when I wasn't looking (well, I was looking, with a mixture of interest and pride). She dove under the table and we fed her cheese, reaching down until we felt the cheese was gone. She surfaced and wrestled her stuffed frog. It was a nice dinner, but when we left it was still light out. And we were worn out from prying olive pits out of Zoë's fists, searching under the table for her pinned frog, blowing on cheese.

We have good friends in Oakland who love to cook. He's a classical guitarist who is neurotic about practicing scales, she's a graduate student in English who is trying to write her dissertation. To procrastinate they make pizza. We have dinner with them often. There's a whole process of rolling dough, spreading olive oil, chopping garlic. Zoë sits on our laps and gets covered in flour. After half an hour we take Zoë to their bedroom and make a spot on the bed and she sleeps. It's fun in the middle of eating pizza and drinking my friends' expensive wine to tiptoe down the hall and crack the door and make sure she's still sleeping.

But as much as I like eating at our friends' house, it feels like an admission of defeat (and we are going through all their wine). I miss eating out with Zoë when she was a handbag. I miss eating out when it's dark. I wouldn't mind missing the carp in a certain sushi restaurant's bathroom. I fear we will soon throw in the napkin entirely and surrender ourselves to an inedible future of high chairs and mac and cheese.

So when we return to Chez Panisse, I am apprehensive. We are bringing the time bomb. Joining us are two of my friends, one a journalist with a red beard, the other a novelist who just sold his first book. It's a warm spring evening. We walk up the stairs into the café, which is bustling and familiar and glowing. Waiters glide past, smells slide past. The maître d' recognizes or doesn't recognize us again. I look for the side table that is Alice Waters's but don't see her and we settle into a wooden booth.

As in the fall, Zoë nurses. But this time she does not sleep. She sits in Elise's lap and looks around. She mouths bread and butter. She plays with one of my friends' eyeglasses, the other's beard, both of their noses. For appetizers we get an avocado salad, baked Sonoma goat cheese, the nettle frittata. Zoë eats avocado. She tastes the frittata, makes a face, and dives under the table. Then she comes up in my lap. I look at Zoë, then at my watch, and realize she has made it past thirty minutes. I'm shocked in a hold-my-breath-in sort of way. Maybe it's my friends, who are constantly making faces at her, maybe it's the bubbling of Chez Panisse, maybe it's her maturing temperament, but so far Zoë seems to be in one piece. She's no longer the handbag she was when we were here in the fall, nor is she the bomb from a few weeks ago. She's something else. It's like a small friendly gourmand has crawled out of the handbag and is tumbling around in our laps and tasting the food.

Before our meals come I carry Zoë around the café. She pokes the Panisse posters and stares at the chefs chopping garlic. I stare at the desserts. We return to the booth and our food arrives, pasta and fish and Niman Ranch beef. As the plates make their way around the table so we can taste everyone else's dinner, we talk about the latest publishing gossip, which writer said what about another writer, who's sleeping with whom, and we tell the old jokes and stories we've all heard before, and tell older stories and other things we have not heard before, and the evening sort of evolves and the food and wine keep circling and we slowly approach that feeling of *hygge*. We just happen to have a child with us.

As we wipe our plates clean I take another walk with Zoë. I head outside and stand on the sidewalk and look at the menu and I'm hit with the feeling that I have been here before.

When Zoë was a week old we walked down the hill to the local deli. It was our first dinner out. After a few minutes Zoë started crying and I took her outside to calm her. I walked to Chez Panisse to read the menu. There was a man standing in front of the menu and he was carrying a baby, too. We stood side by side looking at the menu. The man, who had been eating inside the restaurant and come out when his baby started crying, shook his head and grumbled that he couldn't believe he was out here looking in.

Standing in the same place tonight I guess I'm that father half a year later. But I'm not. I don't mind that we're out here. I've had a glass of wine or three so I'm not minding anything. In fact, I sort of like it. I like reading the menu: "Terra Firma Farm purple and green asparagus with *sauce gribiche*." Zoë likes grabbing the vines around the menu. Time can wait.

I'm looking forward to returning to the café, looking forward to sliding back into the wooden booth and seeing what I missed. Maybe my friends and Elise have added layers to the conversation, maybe they're telling bad jokes. Maybe they got another bottle of wine and dessert is on the table. I like knowing I will soon be back in that glow, with good friends and my daughter around me, and savoring this thought is a dish I cannot eat but one that fills me anyway.

—*what we take with us*—

A few weeks ago, Elise cut Zoë's hair. It was Zoë's sixth haircut in her first nine months; she has a lot of hair. With each curl that fell to the floor I felt nostalgic for the baby she used to be. She's growing up, it's unstoppable. At one point she wrapped her fingers around my forefinger and smiled at me and as I looked into her eyes I was struck with sadness.

I remember times when I was a kid and talking with my father—about a football game I played, or my rant of the day—and I'd see him smiling back at me and wonder why he let me meander this way. I think now that he was just happy to listen to me, this thing he helped bring into this world. He was with me and that was enough. I wonder if in these moments my father was not really seeing me, or he was seeing more of me than I knew: the baby me, the tod-dler me, the continuum of my life and his.

No man in his twenties thinks he will die. Then, in the instant a father first kisses his newborn's forehead this feeling of immortality evaporates. There's an in-the-gut awareness in giving life that life itself is not so long. Death is certain. The baby proves it. As the baby grows into a child and beyond, this is confirmed again and again. When I brought Zoë to the farm where I grew up, I felt genera-tions shifting. I was no longer the boy who grew up on this farm. I was a man bringing his child to where he had been a child. Your child is your mortality looking at you.

And yet, to look into your child's eyes is also to experi-ence something close to eternal. When I look at Zoë she is so beautiful to me it makes me ache. I look at her and am floored. So these feelings, of wonder and sadness both, meet in parents' eyes when they see their child.

Looking at Zoë now I realize I have a big dreamy smile on my face, just like my father. I couldn't be happier to watch her grow up. But I also feel desperately sad because I will not be around to see her grow old, and because I want her to grow old. I have only one goal for Zoë: that she out-live me.

Maybe I'm thinking about change and death because we're moving to Chicago and I'm worried I may freeze there. And, it's tough leaving California. To remember our home I walk with Zoë around the neighborhood and sketch the things I described to her on our evening walks when she was an infant: the black-and-white cat, the oak tree growing through the fence, the view of the bay. I'm thinking those fall walks could be a children's book. On these spring walks, though, Zoë gets in the way, grabbing my pencil and my notebook, climbing on my head. I end up sketching with her slung backward over my shoulder, her feet in my face as she pounds my rear with both fists.

I say goodbye to favorite places. I walk to Codornices Park and ride with Zoë down the slide under the oak tree that was too steep just a month before. I take her for a rumble in the Willard Park dog run. I ask the workers at the Cheese Board to make blueberry scones for my last day. We go to the Parkway Theater for a movie that is forgettable but has lots of car chases. We drive to Point Reyes and to South Beach, and though Zoë stays tucked inside Elise's sweatshirt she is able to see her naked father jumping into the big waves. I drive to secondhand stores and sell another batch of stuffed bunnies.

The last time I go to Royal Coffee I'm in a hurry and double-park next to a big shiny Harley. I run past a two-hundred-and-fifty-pound biker with leather pants and wife-beater tank top who says, "What, are you *crazy*?!" but I keep going by the outside tables and the regulars who will be sitting at them in the days and months and years ahead. Then I get my coffee and run out past the same biker, who repeats his query about my sanity and I throw my arms wide and give him my best *wanna-fuck-with-me?* gesture, the sort of gesture only a guy who's halfway inside a car and leaving town the next day can give.

Elise and I go to Chez Panisse that night without Zoë. We talk about what we will miss (running on grass and green hills in January) and what we won't (people wearing their bike helmets in the aisles of Berkeley Bowl). I will miss, more than anything, this part of my life when I became a father. We talk about how we came to California as a couple and how we are leaving with this girl. As we talk I am trying to fix this place in my memory, to make it stick.

I have a memory of learning to stand. I picture an open dishwasher door I was leaning against, trying to reach the family cat I had chased inside. Of course, maybe I don't remember this. Maybe I remember a photograph my mother showed me years later. I hope Zoë will remember something about California.

I tell Elise about a rainy day last month. I'd gone to the park with Zoë inside my jacket and only her head poking out. It was wild—the umbrella blew inside out—and as I splashed through the puddles Zoë fell asleep with raindrops rattling above us. I love that sound. It's the kind of sound that I hope could bury into her subconscious alongside the feeling of being held and warm, and resurface in some deeply known but inexplicable way when it rains again years later.

As we lick our plates clean I wonder something further, something strange and self-centered. If our children are our mortality, they're also our attempt at immortality. I'm not saying I will live through Zoë. But maybe, like the sound of the rain, I will remain in her memory, then in her stories about those memories, and in that form I will last and be passed along to her children and their children long after I am gone.

In the morning I take Zoë next door to see our neighbor's Alexander Calder mobile. I'd been meaning to do this for a long time. In fact, I've been saying ever since first seeing the mobile that the day I left California I would take it with me. That day is here, so here's my chance. Who's going to miss a small mobile anyway? It is lovely. Oblong pieces of metal—black, white, red—turning in the breeze coming through the open windows. Our neighbor lets me reach up and push it, and it flows in perfect balance and countless variations. Zoë stares at it. Will she remember this and take it with her, these flashes of color, this moment, the breath of wind in these hills?

—*full, empty*—

I've convinced an old friend to drive with me cross-country. He lives in Los Angeles, where he is an actor, a violinist, and an usher at Dodger Stadium. When I first met him, freshman year in college, he was trying to make it until Thanksgiving without washing his clothes, for reasons that were unclear to the rest of us. In recent years he and I have made pilgrimages to all-night raves and to see the Green Bay Packers play in the snow. So he was the first person I thought of when I knew I had to drive our car east. Elise is flying later with Zoë and we're meeting in New York in a roundabout trip to our new home in Chicago.

After picking up my friend at the Oakland Airport and packing his violin alongside my football in the trunk, we head out. We talk about women, baseball, football, and women. We drive all night, only stopping on the outskirts of a small Western town to watch a Little League baseball game. Towns click past: Reno, Elko, Wells. We sleep in the front seats of the car and wake up looking at mountains. In Salt Lake we brush our teeth in the parking lot of a big church. Up the road we take photos of ourselves in front of a bull-semen collection ranch. In the Tetons we walk around a lake, in Yellowstone we take photos of tourists taking photos of a moose. I've brought peanut butter and we spread it on tortillas with my Swiss Army Knife until the blade gets stuck and then we spread it with our fingers. We stop rarely, peeing in cups we toss out the window. Crossing over the Stillwater River in Montana I check my messages and there's one from Elise, with Zoë babbling in the background. It's strange to hear their voices out here under the big sky. I haven't been thinking about them at all.

In the fall, when Elise took Zoë back east to a conference, I had a great time by myself. After dropping them at the airport I drove straight to Royal Coffee and sat outside and read the paper like the idlest café regular. I went to my touch-football game early and played for almost three hours. I took a nap, drove to Palo Alto, and picked up a friend and headed over the hills and swam in the ocean. In the evening I ate at a sushi bar alone, then went to a late-night movie before coming home to a big empty bed.

I woke up late to another day that brought more of the same. Dawdling at the Cheese Board, browsing at Black Oak Books, doing all the errands I'd been meaning to do for months. I'd look at my watch and realize I had nowhere to be. In the afternoon I sat outside Royal Coffee again and read the entire Sunday *Times*. As I was leafing through Arts & Leisure, occasionally coming up for air to watch people walking past, I saw a family, the father with a baby girl in his arms, and my mood of Sunday afternoon well-being was interrupted by a stab of guilt. I was enjoying this too much.

I could have chosen to fly East and help Elise. However, since I would have been staying with Elise's parents in a crowded hotel room, I decided, in the same way that I choose not to dance naked on a beehive, to stay home. But I had the choice. The fact that I have options, that I don't have lactating breasts, that I am a man, means in some profound sense that I can run away. Being a father is an invitation to selfishness.

Since Zoë was born I find I've been selfish in small and not pretty ways. Mostly I'm selfish with time. When we eat out I'll let Elise take Zoë outside while I pay the check, and it's because it gives me the two extra minutes to sit and enjoy my coffee. I'll come home five minutes late from an errand when I could have been on time. I'll stay in the shower one delicious minute more before I have to come out and take care of my daughter. It's not good. I know I'm not respecting Elise's time, being the thief of it in fact, but it doesn't stop me. This makes me sort of squirrelly, something I'd rather not admit. As this family walked past me at the café I pushed these thoughts down and dove back into the paper and read every last bit of it, holding on as the shadows of the day stretched across me.

Being alone and being selfish about it has its merits, though. When I sketch I am alone. I wrote a sketchbook about California a few years ago. I spent months crisscrossing the state, sleeping in the car and waking up on a ranch to sketch some cattle branding, then heading off to find my next adventure. It was a deeply happy and solitary experience, one I couldn't have shared with anyone. And the beauty of traveling alone was that after a few sweaty days I was also filled with the longing to come home. I couldn't wait to see Elise, and she was happy to see me, too, after I took a shower.

My friend and I have not showered. In fact, somewhere outside Reno I decide to wear the same T-shirt the entire trip. We pull over at the Little Big Horn battlefield and walk around, keeping our eyes at our feet for rattlesnakes. Heading south alongside the Little Big Horn River in the last light of the day, my friend sees a train on the other side of the valley inching its way toward us a mile away, and he leans his body out the window as I hold on to his legs and he pumps his fist up and down and the conductor sees him and sounds his horn and it echoes through the whole valley. We eat at a sports bar in Sheridan, Wyoming. I miss another message from Elise. Her voice sounds distant. We drive into the night and pull the car to the side of the road and sleep.

In the morning we are in South Dakota. We drive through the Rosebud Indian Reservation and don't say much, then into Nebraska, pulling over to throw the football on a dirt road next to ponds filled with tall white birds. We stop in Lincoln and look for a special cabbage sandwich my friend heard about called the Runza. We don't find the Runza. On our way out of town we walk to the stadium where the Cornhuskers play and I throw my football inside—we hear it bounce and echo down the concrete steps—then head back into the night. The car has taken on a certain familiarity, a mess of clothes and maps bunched together that nonetheless does not keep us from knowing where everything is. We pick up a Cubs game on the radio.

Towns click past: Booneville, Des Moines, Moscow. We stop for gas.

It's two in the morning, pitch-black and chilly. Even though we've been on the road for hours, I am wide awake, porous. Stars above, the blinking lights from a farm on the horizon, the whoosh of trucks on the highway. The interstate is my ocean and I am a captain on this boat. Then, as I'm standing there, my hand on the pump, I see the grinning face of a tiger on a poster in the window of the gas station. As I look at this tiger, the familiar feeling creeps up on me that has always crept up on me after a certain number of days on all the trips I have ever taken. I'm missing home. I'm adrift, too far from shore. And while this feeling has always been about Elise I feel it now for Zoë, too. I miss her in my arms, pointing out something I think she might like. The space within my arms feels emptier than ever except for this nozzle that I am holding that does not respond when I point and say, "Look. Tiger."

Someday I will travel with my daughter. Someday we will take a road trip. We'll drive out on a Western highway and see mountains and moose, a sky full of stars. Maybe she'll bring a sketchbook and draw, too. Maybe, of course, she'll be bored. And maybe she won't want to leave home, or at least not with me. But I will ask.

I walk inside and pay for the gas—the kid with the Iowa

Hawkeye hat doesn't look up from his magazine—and my friend and I push back into the night, sleeping in the front seats again and waking up in a cornfield smoky with morning mist. I hope I'm still taking road trips when I'm eighty.

When I see Zoë at the curb at J.F.K. there are two seconds when she doesn't take me in. Then she flips out, her face bursting as she shouts, "*Ta da!*" I am so happy. I'm also flustered. We were stuck in traffic on the George Washington Bridge, standing still for an hour and watching the planes—one of which was carrying Elise and Zoë, no doubt—as they passed overhead. After dropping my friend and his violin off on a corner in the Bronx, I sped through Brooklyn with the windows rolled down to air out the car, thinking for a moment about changing my shirt before deciding not to.

As I load Zoë and Elise and the bags into the car at the curb at J.F.K., a traffic officer curtly tells me to move it and I lose it, getting up in his face and screaming, "*Back! The Fuck! Off!*" All my stress of being late, of being away for five days, all the guilt I have about being by myself and enjoying it, are let loose in a sputtering outburst at this surprised Pakistani traffic officer. To the officer's credit he sees the baby, sees that he is dealing with a crazy man, a smelly man, a father, and he puts up his hands and walks away. I owe him an apology. But as I drive out of the airport, that is the last thing on my mind. I'm staring in the rearview at Elise and Zoë as they sit together in the backseat, breathing them in, looking at them with such a desperate sense of relief, the wild kiss-the-ground relief of having made it home.

— on our own —

Our new apartment is on the second floor of a graystone on a small street a few blocks from Lake Michigan. There are three parks nearby and in one of them is a zoo. The apartment is long, with wooden floors and crooked doors, and wide windows that look down to the street. Zoë's room is in the front. A maple tree is outside her window and she can look at it while on her back getting changed.

She hasn't been on her back much recently. When we were out East she took her first steps. Now she's careening all over, crashing into the boxes that have just arrived from California. Boxes are everywhere. Zoë stumbles among them like a blind rat in a maze, bumping into cardboard and falling down. The sound of boxes opening, and of Elise and me calling to ask where we packed the hammer, is punctuated by the sound of Zoë's rear end hitting the floor with a thump.

The only thing at all organized in the apartment is sound. I'm hammering pieces of wood together: a desk for Elise, shelves for Zoë, a table for Elise. I screw together a crib and hang Zoë's mobile above it. But with each mis-shapen piece of furniture I build, and each unnecessary trip to Home Depot I take, I know I am delaying. I'm trying to put off the inevitable, which is Monday, when *I start taking care of Zoë full time.*

I'm worried. I've always played with Zoë and taken her for walks to the park. But I've always been able to pass her off to Elise after an hour or two, always known that Elise was nearby if either Zoë or I fell apart. What would happen when the nearest responsible person was *me*? It's not just that Zoë could get hurt. I worry she'll have some emotional need I won't know how to meet.

I also worry we'll get tired of each other. Her with me, me with her. Elise will be gone from eight in the morning until late in the afternoon. At the most practical level, what will I do with Zoë until then? What's the plan? The day suddenly feels desperately long, a desert of time I'm staring across. And there's nothing I can do to avoid crossing this desert besides trying to convince Elise to let me build another wobbly table for her.

"Have fun, you two," says Elise from the door. She's smiling, but her expression betrays what I know is wrenching for her, leaving her daughter for the first time for a whole day. Zoë's and my expressions, on the other hand, betray everything. If I could see through Elise's eyes I can't imagine she'd ever see two more desperate-looking people, both of us prone on the floor, pleading. "You're leaving me with *her*?" "You're leaving me with *him*?" Then Elise is gone with the click of the door behind her. "Okay," I say to Zoë, staring at her for a minute. "Okay."

We've enrolled in classes to fill the time. Our first is a music class at the Old Town School of Folk Music. Zoë sits in my lap and stares wide-eyed at the teacher and his guitar as if he were torturing a cat with each strum of his strings. Zoë stares at the other toddlers, too. They're boisterous and big. When she stands the top of her head comes up to their chins. Though Zoë spends most of class in my lap, she's not entirely comfortable with me, either. I imagine she's looking for Elise, wishing she would walk through the door and stop her pain, and the cat's. In the afternoon she takes the longest nap. Elise surprises us by coming home early and I go jump in the lake.

The following morning when Elise says goodbye I am able to respond standing up. Then Zoë and I go to a swim class at the Y.M.C.A. The rubber ducks may as well be sharks. The pool is frigid and Zoë sticks to me like a barnacle and shivers afterward in a big towel. As we walk home she trips on the sidewalk and skins her knee then buries her head in my chest and bawls. She stays in my arms for ten minutes. While usually she doesn't turn to me when she's hurt, right now I'm all she's got.

After a few days of classes, I have an idea. We go to the local bike store and I buy a baby seat for my bike, and a helmet for Zoë. It's the smallest helmet possible but it's still too big—she looks like a mushroom—and it falls off when we start biking and I put it back on and look around to see if anyone noticed. We bike to the lake. We go to the North Avenue beach and sit in the sand, building castles and knocking them down. Zoë gets sand in her eyes and cries and we wade into the water and wash them out. Afterward we share an ice cream sandwich. On our way home a semi passes us and I teach Zoë to pump her arm up and down so that the driver pulls the handle on his horn.

In the next weeks we bike everywhere. We bike to a water park, we bike to the library, we bike to the zoo. We watch the lions, then ride a tiger on the zoo carousel, Zoë in my lap and holding tight to the pole.

Some days we have no plans. We walk to Oz Park and sit in the flower garden and look at books. Zoë flips through hers and I read mine—a history of Chicago—pausing to tell her we may be sitting in what used to be a marsh, that the Indian name for the garlic that grew here was *chi-goug*, and that *Chicagou* means "the wild-garlic place."

We lie on our backs and watch the clouds. I read that L. Frank Baum, who lived nearby, was persuaded by his children on his way out one stormy morning to stay and tell them a story, which is how "Oz" began. As we watch the thunderclouds looming above us, the Wicked Witch of the West makes sense. Then the clouds open and it starts to rain and we wave goodbye to the statue of the Cowardly Lion and rush home to warmth and lunch.

Other days our plans dissolve. Biking to the zoo one morning Zoë sees something and starts thumping me on the back. It's a tree full of crab apples. We stop, and I hold Zoë up into the branches as if she were one of those hooked apple pickers. We stay under the tree, arranging and rear-ranging piles of apples, and I forget where we were going. I'm only shaken out of my reverie an hour later on our way home by the loud honk of a truck horn right next to my ear. Zoë, in the seat behind me, has taken to pumping her fist at semis when I'm not looking.

The following day on the way to the beach we go to

the zoo. We don't see animals, though, and just ride the carousel, which Zoë tries to ride with no hands. At the zoo store she wraps her arms around a tiger that is bigger than she is and it somehow comes with us back to the apartment.

"Have fun, you two," Elise must have said. But Zoë and I are in the back room looking for our bike helmets and don't hear her. Elise pokes her head back in the door and says, "You guys okay?" We look up and I say, "Yeah, sorry. You have fun, too." Zoë finds her helmet and puts it on backward and races toward the door before thumping into the wall.

Elise isn't coming home as early. I know that she was coming home at first to rescue us, to rescue me. I know that she was coming home to save herself, too. That this was heartbreaking, and that as it got easier for me it got harder for her, at least before it didn't.

I will never replace Elise. The intensity of the look she and Zoë share when they see each other at the end of the day is not replicable. But I'm needed. I'm there for Zoë in music class, which is still worrisome, and at the Y.M.C.A. pool, which is still cold. I'm there when she skins her knee. For what Zoë needs most from me is to come down to her level. Crouching beside her on the beach and sifting grains of sand through our hands and looking at bugs. Our time lengthens, focused as we are on the small and the mundane, and both of us are able to give the other what we need. It's as if that desert of time became less daunting as soon as I saw we could just sit in the sand.

There's a portrait of Abraham Lincoln on the landing outside our door. It doesn't belong to us, and at first I thought it was tacky. Now I like it. Lincoln was from Illinois, after all. Every time Zoë and I go out we say goodbye to Abe. He, in oil, always has the same serene expression. We give him a smile and a big wave as I call out, "Bye, Abe." We head past Oz Park and there's the statue of the Cowardly Lion and we wave at him, too, "Bye, Lion." Then we're off on our own, to whatever we bring to the day and whatever it brings to us. Our day is packed.

—in the land of mothers—

Someone stole our bike. It was old and beat-up, with grimy gears and peeling paint, but it was ours. It was how Zoë and I got around. The baby seat was taken, too. It's unrealistic to expect that whoever stole the bike would take the baby seat off and leave it, but that would have been nice. Compounding the theft was that it was my fault. I'd run upstairs to pass Zoë to Elise at the end of a ride and left the bike leaning against the stoop.

Zoë is coming up on her first birthday. Elise and I have started planning her party. We're wondering whether we should bake a chocolate cake or a carrot cake, have a picnic in the park or in the apartment, whether we should get her a doll. These are the questions in the front of my mind. In the back of my mind, in the cluttered back rooms one rarely shows to visitors, I'm hung up on the bike's theft. I'm upset at whoever did this, and at myself for letting it happen. I'm obsessing about how to protect my daughter from the world. Specifically, I'm obsessing about how to protect her from boys.

Blond boys in blue button-down shirts have been knocking down my daughter. Zoë isn't perfect, but when she approaches another toddler and holds out a toy, or reaches her hand to one of his, I think she's trying to connect. When they reach out their hand I think they're trying to connect with a punch. I'm exaggerating, somewhat, but when does a parent step in?

A few weeks ago we walked across Oz Park to our local toy store. They have a train table which toddlers play around. Zoë was standing at the table holding a caboose when a three-year-old boy ran past us and over Zoë, knocking her to the floor before continuing on his way with the caboose. He ran back and was heading for Zoë again when I pinned him against the train table with my hip. His feet left the ground and kept moving and he looked like Wile E. Coyote running off a cliff. I whispered, "*Watch out for the girl*," then let him down and he raced off, a look of surprise on his face. When I sheepishly told Elise that night, she shook her head and said, "Great, you're beating up on three-year-olds."

Was I becoming the overly protective father? Maybe it was because I was spending more time with Zoë this summer, or because Zoë was engaging more with her surroundings. While I knew getting knocked down was part of growing up, I also knew how I felt when I saw my daughter fall. I wanted to save her.

When we first came to Chicago we went to Bauler Park, the nearest playground to our house. It's small and shaded and packed with toddlers and their nannies. I always brought a soccer ball but inevitably some unsupervised toddler grabbed it from Zoë with a push, shouted "*Yach!*" and waddled into the bushes. The nannies stayed on the benches telling stories and I ended up negotiating between the toddlers. I started bringing two balls, but that just made it so I had to referee multiple fights.

After a week of this I decided to change playgrounds. We started going to the playground in Oz Park. It had bigger kids but also more of the people I thought would be more involved in the control of the children: mothers. The place was packed with mothers. The first time I went I was the only male except for the homeless guys playing chess at the tables outside the playground.

I approached one group of mothers at the swings. As I pushed Zoë, I listened. The mothers, blonde and put together, were talking to one another about their kitchen remodeling projects, how hard their husbands worked, and when they were moving to the suburbs. Sometimes they put their children down and talked at them, too. "Connor, look at how well *Olivia* is walking! Oh, *Connor*." A look would come over Connor's face of such shame—he couldn't understand the words but he could understand the tone— that I imagined he'd love to take a swing at his mother, if only he could get over to her.

Zoë wasn't getting knocked down, though. The aggression here was verbal, and directed at one's own. We went to the Oz Park playground every morning for a while. I'd push Zoë in the swings and listen to the same mothers have the same conversation. And though I joined in, too, smiling politely and asking questions and sharing stories, I could never shake the feeling that I'd walked into some small South Sea island village and had sidled up to the pot and asked what was cooking.

I just wasn't part of the culture. Underneath the outward smiles, the mothers viewed me, I think, with a bit of suspicion. Maybe it was my unshaven face or my shorts. Maybe it was the fact that I was here in the middle of the day, which meant I didn't have a real job. Or maybe, any man at a playground, even if he had a baby, couldn't quite be trusted. There was an ovary-level nonacceptance.

I knew that if I put in the months and the years, as with any relationship, these mothers might eventually open up and tell me the fertility rights and the secrets of the tribe, but part of me resented that I would have to. I'm *already* a parent. I got my membership when Zoë was born, I thought.

It also turned out the mothers weren't in control of their children any more than the nannies. I'd missed this because the boys had been in the swings, plotting and waiting for the right opportunity. One morning after some unmemorable swinging, the mothers and I walked to the slides. As we were helping the children up the ladder one of the boys toddled forward and kicked Zoë in the back.

"Whoops!" said his mother. Then, in that half-embarrassed parental whisper, "Oh, *Ethan*. That's not nice," as she flapped her arms at her son who now was using Zoë's head as the first rung of the ladder. I stood there shocked. I didn't do anything, though that Rodney King line "Can we all get along?" did pass through my mind. Finally I picked up Zoë. As I plucked wood chips out of her hair and shared that *it's okay* look with the mother, I was left only with the question of why this time I had been so slow to respond.

In the following days there was more stomping from Ethan and his gang. Even Connor, who had learned to walk by now, was getting in on the action and making up for lost time. Since all the boys wore blue I started thinking of them as the Crips. The Crips' mothers weren't that concerned when their child was the aggressor, but if another child, from the Bloods on the other side of the playground, came over and whacked their little Crip kid, the Crip mom would scoop up her son and shoot a glare at the offender's mother that would momentarily freeze the humid summer air.

After the morning gang activity in the wood chips the mothers would gather up their kids and walk to the flower garden next to the playground. They'd arrange blankets in the shade and open bags filled with snacks and juice and Diet Cokes. Then they'd sit in a circle, laughing and smiling and sharing the secrets, no doubt, leaving Zoë and me swinging.

At night I complained to Elise that being a parent would be better if it weren't for mothers. She didn't say anything.

I decided I was done with mothers, done with playgrounds. We would be fine on our own. I walked with Zoë to a pond on the other side of the zoo. We sat at the edge and I pointed out a great blue heron standing motionless in the shallows, the turtle with its head pulled tight into its shell. On our way home one day it started to rain, then pour. I huddled under a tree then took off my shirt and wrapped it around Zoë and ran. I looked foolish, I bet, scurrying shirtless through the rain. I certainly felt foolish. As I ran I couldn't help thinking, what am I protecting Zoë from, exactly? She *likes* the playground. She likes the swings and slides. She likes the other children, even the boys.

I talked with Elise again that night. She, the psychologist, said I was trying to distinguish myself. I was trying to distinguish myself from other parents and expressing my ambivalence about being a parent, which manifested itself in my feelings of alienation (I lost her at some point).

I did understand that the mothers at Oz Park had gotten under my skin. It wasn't just that they were their own tribe. They had something I didn't. They had assurance. They were comfortable as parents. And though I knew these mothers must feel ambivalence, too, and probably shared this when I wasn't around, it did not show. They seemed as strong and impregnable as a herd of cows facing down a dog, while I was yapping around and veering from the extremes of pinning a toddler against a train table to letting my child get used as a ladder. These mothers would never wonder how to protect their child, they just would. They had no doubt; I was full of it.

After Elise and I stopped analyzing my indistinguishedness, she said that Zoë, once we helped her with the skills she needed to stand up for herself, would be fine. I still wondered how she could stand up for herself if she was lying on her back.

The next morning I returned to the Oz Park playground. As I approached I could see the Crips running amok and tipping over toy trucks. The mothers were standing by the swings, unperturbed as usual. I put Zoë in a swing and began to push. The mothers gave me big welcoming smiles and we talked about our favorite kitchen appliance, our hardworking husbands, our impending move to the suburbs. I'd almost missed them.

Then Zoë and I sat and rolled a soccer ball back and forth. Out of the corner of my eye I noticed one of the Crips angling toward us. So I leaned in to Zoë and whispered the words that Elise and I had discussed the night before. "If you want to share your ball with him you can. But if he grabs it say '*No!*'" Then I added something that Elise and I had not discussed. "And if he pushes you, kick him *there,*" I said, pointing at his shins. I was distinguishing myself as a parent after all.

I have one friend in Chicago who's a father. He's a huge Cubs fan and we've gone to a bunch of baseball games this summer with our daughters. Day games are our day care and Wrigley Field our playground. While the girls sit on our laps and play with balloons, we drink beer and watch out for foul balls. Then we guide the girls on wobbly walks down the aisles. Sometimes I watch the fans around us, whose concerns don't revolve around diapers and day care, and feel such wishful camaraderie. These people seem so carefree, so pleasant, so drunk. I look at them and think how much I still struggle being a parent. My worries from the fall are still there. I don't want to be in this group "parent." And then, I do. I want to belong. With a sharp intake of breath I remember the feeling I had watching the women in Oz Park walking off together to the flower garden: I wished I were a mother.

As I let my breath out, I also realize that I no longer struggle with being the parent to this child in my lap. Any worries about being her father have dissipated to the point where I don't even remember what they were. It is as if Zoë has always been with me. Being *her* parent is without doubt. And that is the most relieving thing in the world.

I've moved on to other worries: how to fit in as a father, how to protect my child. How to know when to help her stand and when to let her fall through the air and into the world. Just the impossible particulars of parenting.

When the Crip in the Oz Park playground reached for

her soccer ball, Zoë handed it to him. After a minute she reached for the ball back and when the boy didn't give it, she toddled up within an inch of his chin, shot him the sternest one-year-old frown, and barked something unintelligible which I like to think was "*Back!*" The startled boy placed the ball in her arms and ran off, to the next girl whose ball or heart he could steal. I was so proud of Zoë. She'd grow up, even if I couldn't.

Our new bike is ready. It is plain and black, with a sturdy lock and a baby seat on the back. It will be perfect once it's beaten up a bit. Zoë picks out a helmet covered in pigs and sheep and goats as I attach the chrome Zen Japanese bell a friend from Berkeley sent me. We bike home by way of the toy store. While Zoë is over by the train table, playing alongside some other toddlers, I get her a doll, and a bulldozer. Then we walk across the park, the toys in the baby seat and Zoë toddling in front.

Today is Zoë's birthday. This girl who came out wide-eyed and bloody has made it one year. Elise and I are one year old in a way, too. It is amazing to remember what Elise did last year and all that has happened since, and it strikes me as never before that today is a *birth* day. We were hoping for a picnic in the park but a summer downpour keeps us inside. Zoë rumbles through the apartment with a pizza crust in her fist. We put a candle on top of the carrot cake and she reaches to grab the flame at the same moment Elise blows it out. Zoë is one.

A few nights ago there was a huge thunderstorm. Cracking thunderclaps, flashes of lighting. The apartment walls lit up white. As the thunder came closer and closer, rolling across the outskirts of Chicago, across the farms of Illinois, across the plains and what felt like the entire country, it was both sweet and thrilling with us safe inside our new home. But when the first lightning strike hit—the first that seemed to hit inside the house—I felt my legs getting out of bed before my mind: *must check on girl*. She was fine. Her face calm and tilted to the side, buried in her stuffed tiger. One hand up in a wave, quiet and dreaming as the outside world crashed around her. And I thought, I will never be able to protect her, but I will try, and this will haunt me always I know, as she grows and changes and eventually leaves and becomes a woman, the years playing out in front of us.

—the dog—

I didn't see it coming, though it was right there in front of me. The dog, napping and unpredictable. Zoë, walking toward him to give him a hug. Me, sitting and listening to Elise and our friends' voices drifting in and out of the kitchen along with the chopping of tomatoes for sand-wiches and the creaking of the screen door to the porch. The rhythms of a summer day.

We are up in Maine. We've come here with two couples —college friends of ours—and one energetic dog. We're staying in a wooden cabin on a lake that stretches to the opposite shore then up into big-cloud skies. No houses are visible from the porch—the only visitors the solitary eagle that sometimes flies overhead, a family of loons beyond the dock. There are no phones. We're near the Canadian border, far from the nearest town. Some years ago I brought Elise here and we canoed to the middle of the lake and I asked her to marry me. She turned and said, *"Are you joking?!"* and took off her clothes and jumped into the water either because she was happy or because she wanted to escape while she still could. On my desk at home I have a black-and-white photograph of Elise at another time, just out of the water and standing on the dock. Above Zoë's changing table I put a map of the lake, and sometimes when changing her I would tell her how I would take her to this lake in Maine when she was older and she would love it.

When the dog reared and bit Zoë on the head, I was actually reaching to pick her up. Everything happened slowly, then quickly: girl leaning, dog snapping, me shouting, the three of us joining in a tangle of limbs and teeth, then separating as I lifted Zoë to see if she was hurt. At first I thought she was okay. "She's okay," I said to Elise, who had raced in from the porch as I raced out. But Zoë was pawing at her head. And then the blood came. It was everywhere. Elise ran to the bathroom and clamped a towel on Zoë's head, taking it off for a moment to reveal two ragged edges of flesh at the hairline, deep and mean, welling with blood. "We need to get her to a hospital, now," someone said. After conferring with our friends and walking out the banging screen door, we got into the car—an afternoon of making the perfect sandwich transformed in an instant—and a minute later were racing on a dirt logging road to the nearest phone, three miles away.

Zoë was hiccuping with shock on Elise's lap. I was driving, a friend sat next to me. We came to the Oquossoc general store. I ran to the pay phone and dialed 911. An operator told me an ambulance would be there in five minutes. When I returned to the car a paramedic—I have no idea where she came from—was examining Zoë's head and telling us that the bleeding had stopped and that the nearest emergency room was in Rumford, forty miles away, and that waiting for the ambulance would just slow us down.

So as the flashing lights of the ambulance pulled into one end of the general store parking lot we were speeding in the other direction in a swirl of dust. I drove fast, but under some control as I reasoned that an accident wouldn't help, and a silence settled over the car. The situation had stabilized, our initial shock worn off. Zoë nursed, coming off Elise's breast at times to cry, and then she slept. Elise sang to her, and when I looked in the rearview I could see Elise was crying, too. Our friend sat next to me in the passenger seat and was silent because it was his dog. I talked. I could tell Zoë would be okay, so I said it. "She's okay. She's going to be fine." I asked if we were okay, then answered for all of us, trying to reassure everyone, trying to sound calm and how I imagined a strong father would sound in such a situation. I kept driving, steering this ship to safe waters as the lakes and forests of Maine swept past looking as beautiful as ever. Half an hour later we pulled up to the hospital in Rumford.

It was a slow day at the Rumford emergency room. A baseball game was playing on the television in the waiting room. The paramedic who helped us in Oquossoc had called ahead and everyone was waiting for the baby who had been bitten by the dog. As we filled out forms, the three of us were joking, the humor that comes after stress: *but you should see the dog!* Even Zoë seemed better. The doctor was young and sharp. He told us what needed to be done and minutes later we had Zoë wrapped and straitjacketed to a wooden board. The doctor cleaned the wound with antiseptic then pushed a needle directly and repeatedly into the wound to numb it. Zoë looked to us, first at Elise and then at me, uncomprehending. Elise held her on one side, me on the other, until her screams became silent screams and nothing came out. It was just the doctor looping dark stitches into her head in the hum of the emergency room. Elise said later that this was the worst part. But the rational part of me knew that this would pass, knew we had to get through it and she would be stitched and safe. Two hours after walk-ing into the emergency room we walked back outside.

I was so thankful Zoë was okay I was almost breathless. She's okay, she's okay, she's okay! As we headed to the car I couldn't stop talking. We drove, slower this time, to the local pharmacy to pick up antibiotics. In the parking lot of the pharmacy, a pharmacy like any other, we got out of the car. Elise held Zoë. My friend got out of the front seat. I was so relieved and wanted him to feel relieved, too. I said, "Are you okay?" He said, "No. No, I'm not."

And then I lost it. I fell apart. I put my arm around my friend and he put his arm around me and we walked across the parking lot, our words overlapping in a rush of how I had been so careless and how his dog had done this to my daughter and how I had done nothing to stop it. I almost killed her. *I was right there.* We stood there holding each other, though at this point he was holding me, and I couldn't stop crying—heaving and not saying much anymore—and Elise came up behind me and I could feel her arms on my back and then I felt her place Zoë in my arms and I was supported on all sides. My head was down and they were holding me and Zoë was between the three of us and I could feel her reaching up to me and touching my face and wondering why her father was crying. We stood there awhile, the pneumatic door of the pharmacy opening and shutting before us.

In our remaining days in Maine we kept to the lake. We sat on the porch and ate sandwiches, and paddled out to an island and picked blueberries and baked pies, doing all the things we had meant to do before what had happened happened. We talked late into the night, sharing stories that often had to do with some disaster that had been narrowly averted. Stories so cringing that all you could do was laugh at them. Our friends were thinking of having children and we talked about that, too, the hope and anxiety that comes with a child. Before going to bed we went outside and watched shooting stars, the Milky Way stretching above us in the black and still sky. We all got closer, though we kept the dog and Zoë apart. After three days our friends left, and Elise and I brought Zoë down to the dock and jumped in the lake before getting on a plane and flying home.

I felt something in that pharmacy in Rumford, something I try not to let the many tellings of this story wash away. We are walking through the store, my friend and I supporting each other down the aisles and drinking the sodas we took from the cooler. We have ordered the antibiotics and are looking now for gauze and Band-Aids. Elise and Zoë are in front of us. Zoë has a bandage on her head covering the stitches that lie on the part of her hair like a barrette. She has one arm around Elise, the other reaching out, and as she points at a photo of a dog on the side of some dog food her face breaks into a big smile and I felt this:

I am in a state of grace. I can do no wrong, even when I have done nothing right. I am drained and full. This child breaks my heart, then fills it. She fills me with love and worry and confusion and desperation that nonetheless come to rest in a place of peace. I am her father, nothing more and nothing less. The father to this child with a dimple on her chin. This person, my daughter.

ACKNOWLEDGMENTS

Thanks to the three friends who worked with me on the writing: to Austin Bunn, for knocking around ideas and breaking it all down; to Janice P. Nimura, for keeping me on track; and to Barney Latimer, whose edits were the type only a friend since birth could give.

Thanks to the many other friends, and relatives, whose conversations helped shape the book: Kevin Delaney, Lisbeth Shepherd, Joshua Spanogle, Mark Holtzen, Daphne Uviller, Sacha Spector, Jordan Henry, Sean Wilsey, Josh Gilbert, Carey Bartell, Clark McKown, Mark Edstrom, Jeff Cappella, and Tremaine Cooper.

Thanks to my own parents for planting in me a love of words and art. Thanks for planting me, too.

I'm grateful to Rob Weisbach for encouraging me to

keep a notebook during my first year as a father. I'm always grateful to my agent Liz Darhansoff for her confidence and instinct.

Thanks to my editor Edward Kastenmeier for his thoughtfulness and care, and special thanks to his baby daughter, whose unwitting presence was essential in making this book come to life. Thank you to Deb Garrison, Dan Frank, Janice Goldklang, Archie Ferguson, Kristen Bearse, Jenna Bagnini, Kate Norris, Leah Heifferon, and everyone at Knopf and Pantheon whose work makes a book.

My thanks to the people and coffee at the Chicago cafés—Intelligentsia, Milk & Honey, The Grind—where I wrote.

Above all, thank you to Elise Cappella, for her enthusiasm throughout, for her faith that writing about our child was something I could do. Thank you for the late-night talks. Thank you for our daughters. To Zoë, and now to Mia, I hope that when you see this book someday you will not be too embarrassed. And maybe, possibly, a bit curious.